easy to make!
Rice & Risottos

Good Housekeeping

easy to make!
Rice & Risottos

COLLINS & BROWN

First published in Great Britain in 2012
by Collins & Brown
10 Southcombe Street
London W14 0RA

An imprint of Anova Books Company Ltd

The Good Housekeeping website is
www.allaboutyou.com/goodhousekeeping

10 9 8 7 6 5 4 3 2 1

ISBN 978-1-908449-22-1

A catalogue record for this book is available from the British
Library.

Reproduction by Dot Gradations Ltd
Printed and bound by Times Offset (M) Sdn. Bhd, Malaysia

This book can be ordered direct from the publisher at
www.anovabooks.com

NOTES

- Both metric and imperial measures are given for the recipes. Follow either set of measures, not a mixture of both, as they are not interchangeable.
- All spoon measures are level.
  1 tsp = 5ml spoon; 1 tbsp = 15ml spoon.
- Ovens and grills must be preheated to the specified temperature.
- Use sea salt and freshly ground black pepper unless otherwise suggested.
- Fresh herbs should be used unless dried herbs are specified in a recipe.
- Medium eggs should be used except where otherwise specified. Free-range eggs are recommended.
- Note that certain recipes, including mayonnaise, lemon curd and some cold desserts, contain raw or lightly cooked eggs. The young, elderly, pregnant women and anyone with an immune-deficiency disease should avoid these, because of the slight risk of salmonella.
- Calorie, fat and carbohydrate counts per serving are provided for the recipes.
- If you are following a gluten- or dairy-free diet, check the labels on all pre-packaged food goods.
- Recipe serving suggestions do not take gluten- or dairy-free diets into account.

Picture Credits
Photographers: Neil Barclay (pages 111, 114 and 117); Martin
Brigdale (pages 37, 40, 43, 47, 64, 65, 66, 79, 80, 81, 85, 89 and
118); Nicki Dowey (pages 32, 33, 35, 38, 39, 41, 42, 45, 48, 49,
50, 53, 63, 67, 72, 75, 76, 77, 78, 86, 92, 94, 97, 98, 99, 101, 109
and 112); Will Heap (pages 51, 62 and 96); Craig Robertson
(Basics photography and pages 34, 54, 58, 59, 60, 69, 82, 84, 95,
102, 106, 115, 119 and 122); Lucinda Symons (pages 87, 100,
108, 116, 125 and 126).
Home Economists: Anna Burges-Lumsden, Joanna Farrow,
Emma Jane Frost, Teresa Goldfinch, Alice Hart, Lucy McKelvie,
Kim Morphew, Aya Nishimura, Katie Rogers, Bridges Sargeson,
Jennifer White and Mari Mererid Williams.
Stylists: Helen Trent and Fanny Ward.

Contents

Foreword

Cooking, for me, is one of life's great pleasures. Not only is it necessary to fuel your body, but it exercises creativity, skill, social bonding and patience. The science behind the cooking also fascinates me, learning to understand how yeast works, or to grasp why certain flavours marry quite so well (in my mind) is to become a good cook.

I've often encountered people who claim not to be able to cook – they're just not interested or say they simply don't have time. My sister won't mind me saying that she was one of those who sat firmly in the camp of disinterested domestic goddess. But things change, she realised that my mother (an excellent cook) can't always be on hand to prepare steaming home-cooked meals and that she actually wanted to become a mother one day who was able to whip up good food for her own family. All it took was some good cook books (naturally, Good Housekeeping was present and accounted for) and some enthusiasm and sure enough she is now a kitchen wizard, creating such confections that even baffle me.

I've been lucky enough to have had a love for all things culinary since as long as I can remember. Baking rock-like chocolate cakes and misshapen biscuits was a right of passage that I protectively guard. I made my mistakes young, so have lost the fear of cookery mishaps. I think it's these mishaps that scare people, but when you realise that a mistake made once will seldom be repeated, then kitchen domination can start.

This Good Housekeeping Easy to Make! collection is filled with hundreds of tantalising recipes that have been triple tested (at least!) in our dedicated test kitchens. They have been developed to be easily achievable, delicious and guaranteed to work – taking the chance out of cooking.

I hope you enjoy this collection and that it inspires you to get cooking.

Meike.

Meike Beck
Cookery Editor
Good Housekeeping

0

The Basics

Cooking rice

Rice is one of the staples of Asian and European cooking. It can be cooked and added as one of the ingredients to a dish or served as the perfect accompaniment to curries, stews and stir-fried dishes. It can also be used cold to make salads, added to stir-fries and soups, cooked with milk or coconut milk and sugar to make sweet desserts, or used in stuffings for meat and vegetables.

Perfect rice

Use 50–75g (2–3oz) raw rice per person – or measure by volume 50–75ml (2–2½fl oz).
If you cook rice often, you may want to invest in a special rice steamer. They are available in Asian supermarkets and some kitchen shops and give good, consistent results.

Cooking rice

There are two main types of rice: long-grain and short-grain. Long-grain rice is generally served as an accompaniment; the most commonly used type of long-grain rice in South-east Asian cooking is jasmine rice, also known as Thai fragrant rice. It has a distinctive taste and slightly sticky texture. Long-grain rice needs no special preparation, although it should be washed to remove excess starch. Put the rice in a bowl and cover with cold water. Stir until this becomes cloudy, then drain and repeat until the water is clear.

Long-grain rice

1 Use 50–75g (2–3oz) raw rice per person; measured by volume 50–75ml (2–2½fl oz). Measure the rice by volume and put it in a pan with a pinch of salt and twice the volume of boiling water (or stock).

2 Bring to the boil. Turn the heat down to low and set the timer for the time stated on the pack. The rice should be al dente: tender with a bite at the centre.

3 When the rice is cooked, fluff up the grains with a fork.

Basmati rice

Put the rice in a bowl and cover with cold water. Stir until this becomes cloudy, then drain and repeat until the water is clear. Soak the rice for 30 minutes, then drain before cooking.

Saffron rice

To serve 8, you will need:

500g (1lb 2oz) basmati rice, 900ml (1½ pints) stock made with 1½ chicken stock cubes, 5 tbsp sunflower or light vegetable oil, salt, ½ tsp saffron, 75g (3oz) blanched almonds and pistachio nuts, coarsely chopped, to garnish (optional).

1 Put the rice into a bowl and cover with warm water, then drain well through a sieve.

2 Put the stock, oil and a good pinch of salt into a pan, then cover and bring to the boil. Add the saffron and the rice.

3 Cover the pan and bring the stock back to the boil, then stir, reduce the heat to low, replace the lid and cook gently for 10 minutes or until little holes appear all over the surface of the cooked rice and the grains are tender. Leave to stand, covered, for 15 minutes.

4 Fluff up the rice with a fork and transfer it to a warmed serving dish. Sprinkle the nuts on top of the rice, if using, and serve.

Thai rice

To serve 6, you will need:

500g (1lb 2oz) Thai rice, handful of mint leaves, salt.

1 Cook the rice and mint in lightly salted boiling water for 10–12 minutes or until tender. Drain well and serve.

Basic risotto

Italian risotto is made with medium-grain arborio, vialone nano or carnaroli rice, which release starch to give a rich, creamy texture. It is traditionally cooked on the hob, but can also be cooked in the oven by adding all the liquid in one go and cooking until the liquid is absorbed.

To serve four, you will need:

1 onion, chopped, 50g (2oz) butter, 900ml (1½ pints) hot chicken stock, 225g (8oz) risotto rice, 50g (2oz) freshly grated Parmesan, plus extra to serve.

1 Gently fry the onion in the butter for 10–15 minutes until very lightly coloured. Heat the stock in a separate pan and keep at a simmer. Add the rice to the butter and stir for 1–2 minutes until well coated.

2 Add a ladleful of stock and stir constantly until absorbed. Add the remaining stock a ladleful at a time, stirring, until the rice is al dente (tender but still with bite at the centre), 20–30 minutes (you may not need all the stock). Stir in the Parmesan and serve immediately with extra cheese.

Making sushi

Japanese sushi is made with special short- or medium-grain rice, which has a higher moisture content and stickier consistency, making it perfect for rolling up inside seaweed to make elegant sushi rolls.

Classic sushi rolls

To make four rolls (24 pieces), you will need 150g (5oz) Japanese sushi rice, 2 tbsp rice vinegar, 4 tbsp mirin (rice wine), 1 tbsp caster sugar, 4 sheets nori (seaweed), 1 tbsp wasabi paste, soy sauce, wasabi and pickled ginger to serve.
For the filling you will need 150g (5oz) smoked salmon, cucumber, 2 large spring onions.

1 Put the rice in a pan with 350ml (12fl oz) cold water. Bring to the boil, cover, and simmer for 10 minutes or until the water has evaporated. Remove from the heat and stir in the vinegar, mirin and sugar. Leave to cool, then fluff up with chopsticks.

2 Cut the salmon into long thin strips. Peel and seed the cucumber and cut into strips. Thinly shred the spring onions.

3 Lay a sheet of nori, shiny side down, in the centre of a sushi mat. Spread a quarter of the rice across two-thirds of the nori.

4 Make an indentation along the top of the rice and spread with a little wasabi paste, then lay a quarter of the salmon, cucumber and spring onion across the width.

5 Using your thumbs to pick up the mat, roll it away from you, pressing gently but firmly on the filling as you roll to make a neat cylinder. Unroll the mat and repeat with the remaining nori and fillings.

6 Wet the blade of a very sharp knife. Trim the ends of each roll, cut each one into three equal-sized pieces, then cut each third in half at an angle. Serve with soy sauce, wasabi and pickled ginger.

Making paella

No two Spanish cooks make this classic dish in exactly the same way and the choice and quantities of ingredients vary from home to home. It is usually made in a large flat pan with a dimpled bottom.

Simple paella

Traditionally, paella is made using a medium-grain rice but this version uses long-grain rice.

To serve six, you will need about 1 litre (1³/₄ pints) chicken stock, a pinch of saffron, 6 boneless, skinless chicken thighs, 5 tbsp extra virgin olive oil, 1 large onion, chopped, 4 large garlic cloves, crushed, 1 tsp paprika, 2 red peppers, sliced, 400g can chopped tomatoes, 350g (12oz) long-grain rice, 200ml (7fl oz) dry sherry, 500g (1lb 2oz) cooked mussels, 200g (7oz) cooked tiger prawns, the juice of ¹/₂ -1 lemon (to taste), salt and ground black pepper, lemon wedges and parsley sprigs to serve.

1 Heat the stock, then add the saffron. Take off the heat and leave to infuse for 30 minutes. Cut each chicken thigh into three pieces.

2 Heat half the oil in a large frying pan and, working in batches, fry the chicken for 3–5 minutes until pale golden brown. Set the chicken aside.

3 Lower the heat slightly and add the remaining oil. Fry the onion for 5 minutes until soft. Add the garlic and paprika and stir for 1 minute. Add the chicken, peppers and tomatoes.

4 Stir in the rice, then add one-third of the stock and bring to the boil. Season with salt and pepper.

5 Reduce heat to a simmer. Cook, uncovered, stirring continuously, until most of the liquid is absorbed.

6 Add the remaining stock a little at a time, allowing the rice to absorb it before adding more. (This should take about 25 minutes.) Add the sherry and cook for another 2 minutes.

7 Add the mussels and prawns with the lemon juice. Stir for 5 minutes. Adjust seasoning and garnish with lemon wedges and parsley.

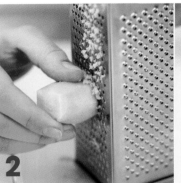

Flavourings

Many stir-fry and curry recipes begin by cooking garlic, ginger and spring onions as the basic flavourings. Spicier dishes may include chillies, lemongrass or a prepared spice paste such as Thai curry paste.

Ginger

1 **Grating** Cut off a piece of the root and peel with a vegetable peeler. Cut off any brown spots.

2 Rest the grater on a board or small plate and grate the ginger. Discard any large fibres adhering to the pulp.

3 **Slicing, shredding and chopping** Cut slices off the ginger and cut off the skin carefully. Cut off any brown spots. Stack the slices and cut into shreds. To chop, stack the shreds and cut across into small pieces.

4 **Pressing** If you just need the ginger juice, peel and cut off any brown spots, then cut into small chunks and use a garlic press held over a small bowl to extract the juice.

Spring onions

Cut off the roots and trim any coarse or withered green parts. Slice diagonally, or shred by cutting into 5cm (2in) lengths then slicing down the lengths, or chop finely, according to the recipe.

Garlic

1 Put the clove on a chopping board and place the flat side of a large knife on top of it. Press down firmly on the flat of the blade to crush the clove and break the papery skin.

2 Cut off the base of the clove and slip the garlic out of its skin. It should come away easily.

3 **Slicing** Using a rocking motion with the knife tip on the board, slice the garlic as thinly as you need.

4 **Shredding and chopping** Holding the slices together, shred them across the slices. Chop the shreds if you need chopped garlic.

5 **Crushing** After step 2, the whole clove can be put into a garlic press. To crush with a knife: roughly chop the peeled cloves with a pinch of salt. Press down hard with the edge of a large knife tip (with the blade facing away from you), then drag the blade along the garlic while still pressing hard. Continue to do this, dragging the knife tip over the garlic.

Chillies

1 Cut off the cap and slit the chilli open lengthways. Using a spoon, scrape out the seeds and the pith.

2 For diced chilli, cut into thin shreds lengthways, then cut crossways.

Cook's Tip

Wash hands thoroughly after handling chillies – the volatile oils will sting if accidentally rubbed into your eyes.

Washing

1 Trim the roots and part of the stalks from the herbs. Immerse in cold water and shake briskly. Leave in the water for a few minutes.

2 Lift out of the water and put in a colander or sieve, then rinse again under the cold tap. Leave to drain for a few minutes, then dry thoroughly on kitchen paper or teatowels, or use a salad spinner.

Using herbs

Most herbs are the leaf of a flowering plant, and are usually sold with much of the stalk intact. They have to be washed, trimmed and then chopped or torn into pieces suitable for your recipe.

Chopping

1 Trim the herbs by pinching off all but the smallest, most tender stalks. If the herb is one with a woody stalk, such as rosemary or thyme, it may be easier to remove the leaves by rubbing the whole bunch between your hands; the leaves should simply pull off the stems.

2 If you are chopping the leaves, gather them into a compact ball in one hand, keeping your fist around the ball (but being careful not to crush them).

3 Chop with a large knife, using a rocking motion and letting just a little of the ball out of your fingers at a time.

4 When the herbs are roughly chopped, continue chopping until the pieces are in small shreds or flakes.

Perfect herbs

- After washing, don't pour the herbs and their water into the sieve, because dirt in the water might get caught in the leaves.
- If the herb has fleshy stalks, such as parsley or coriander, the stalks can be saved to flavour stock or soup. Tie them in a bundle with string for easy removal.

Coriander

Coriander, also known as Chinese parsley, is the most commonly used herb throughout Asia. In Thailand the roots are often used in curry pastes.

1 Trim off any roots and the lower part of the stalks. Immerse in cold water and shake briskly. Leave in the water for a few minutes.

2 Lift out of the water and put in a colander or sieve, then rinse again under the cold tap. Leave to drain for a few minutes, then dry thoroughly on kitchen paper or teatowels, or use a salad spinner.
Note: Don't pour the herbs and their water into the sieve, because dirt in the water might get caught in the leaves.

3 Gather the leaves into a compact ball in one hand, keeping your fist around the ball (but being careful not to crush them). Chop with a large knife, using a rocking motion and letting just a little of the ball out of your fingers at a time.

4 When the herbs are roughly chopped, continue chopping until the pieces are as fine as you need.

Lemongrass

Lemongrass is a popular South-east Asian ingredient, giving an aromatic lemony flavour. It looks rather like a long, slender spring onion, but is fibrous and woody and is usually removed before the dish is served. Alternatively the inner leaves may be very finely chopped or pounded in a mortar and pestle and used in spice pastes.

Onions

1 Cut off the tip and base of the onion. Peel away all the layers of papery skin and any discoloured layers underneath.

2 Put the onion root end down on the chopping board, then, using a sharp knife, cut the onion in half from tip to base.

3 **Slicing** Put one half on the board with the cut surface facing down and slice across the onion.

4 **Chopping** Slice the halved onions from the root end to the top at regular intervals. Next, make two or three horizontal slices through the onion, then slice vertically across the width.

Preparing vegetables

A few basic techniques will help you prepare all kinds of vegetables ready for cooking with rice. For a meal in minutes, look for bags of ready-prepared stir-fry vegetables.

Leeks

As some leeks harbour a lot of grit and earth between their leaves, they need careful cleaning.

1 Cut off the root and any tough parts of the leek. Make a cut into the leaf end of the leek, about 7.5cm (3in) deep.

2 Hold under the cold tap while separating the cut halves to expose any grit. Wash well, then shake dry. Slice, cut into matchsticks or slice diagonally.

Pak choi

Also known as bok choy, pak choi is a type of cabbage that does not form a heart. It has dark green leaves and thick fleshy white stalks, which are sometimes cooked separately.

Cabbage

The crinkly-leaved Savoy cabbage may need more washing than other varieties, because its open leaves catch dirt more easily than the tightly packed white and red cabbage. The following method is suitable for all cabbages, including mild-flavoured Chinese leaves or Chinese cabbage.

1 Pick off any of the outer leaves that are dry, tough or discoloured. Cut off the base and, using a small sharp knife, cut out as much as possible of the tough inner core in a single cone-shaped piece.

2 If you need whole cabbage leaves, peel them off one by one. As you work your way down, you will need to cut out more of the core.

3 If you are cooking the cabbage in wedges, cut it in half lengthways, then cut the pieces into wedges of the required size.

Shredding cabbage

Cut the cabbage into quarters, then slice with a large cook's knife. Alternatively, use the shredding disc of a food processor.

Broccoli

1 Slice off the end of the stalk and cut 1cm (½in) below the florets. Cut the broccoli head in half.

2 Peel the thick, woody skin from the stalks and slice the stalks in half or quarters lengthways. Cut off equal-sized florets with a small knife. If the florets are very large, or if you want them for a stir-fry, you can halve them by cutting lengthways through the stalk and pulling the two halves apart.

Courgettes

Cutting diagonally is ideal for courgettes and other vegetables in a stir-fry.

Wash under the cold tap, dry well and trim the base and the stem. Trim off a piece at the base at a 45° angle, then repeat with the remaining courgette.

Carrots

1 **Paring ribbons** Cut off the ends, then, using a vegetable peeler, peel off the skin and discard. Continue peeling the carrot into ribbon strips.

2 **Slicing** Cut slices off each of the rounded sides to make four flat surfaces that are stable on the chopping board. Hold steady with one hand and cut lengthways into even slices so they are lying in a flat stack. The stack can then be cut into batons or matchsticks.

Asparagus

Cut the asparagus spears about 5cm (2in) from the stalk end, or where the white and green sections meet. Or snap off the woody tip of the stem; it will snap just where the stem becomes tender. Discard the woody end.

Perfect vegetables

Wash vegetables before you cut them up, to retain as many nutrients as possible.

Cook vegetables as soon as possible after you have cut them.

Do not overcook vegetables or they will lose their bright colour, crisp texture and some of their nutrients.

Peppers

Red, green and yellow peppers all contain seeds and white pith which taste bitter and should be removed. **Cut** the pepper in half vertically, discard the seeds and core, then trim away the rest of the white membrane with a small sharp knife. Alternatively, slice the top off the pepper, then cut away and discard the seeds and pith. Cut the pepper into strips or slices.

Celery

To remove the strings in the outer green stalks, trim the ends and cut into the base of the stalk with a small knife; catch the strings between the blade and your thumb. Pull up towards the top of the stalk to remove the string.

Mushrooms

Button, white, chestnut and flat mushrooms are all prepared in a similar way.
Shiitake mushrooms have a hard stalk; cut it off and use for making stock if you like.

1 Wipe with a damp cloth or pastry brush to remove any dirt.

2 With button mushrooms, cut off the stalk flush with the base of the cap. For other mushrooms, cut a thin disc off the end of the stalk and discard. Quarter or slice as needed.

Fennel

1 Trim off the top stems and the base of the bulbs. Remove the core with a small sharp knife if it is tough.

2 The outer leaves may be discoloured and can be scrubbed gently in cold water, or you can peel away the discoloured parts with a knife or a vegetable peeler. Slice or chop the fennel.

Preparing shellfish

Prawns, mussels and small squid are ideal for stir-fries, risottos and Thai curries, because they need brief cooking, otherwise they will become rubbery.

Prawns

Prawns are delicious stir-fried. They can be completely shelled, or you can leave the tail on, but they should be deveined before using.

1 Pull off the head and discard (or put to one side and use later for making stock). Using pointed scissors, cut through the soft shell on the belly side.

2 Prise the shell off, leaving the tail attached. (The shell can also be used later for making stock.)

3 Using a small sharp knife, make a shallow cut along the back of the prawn. Using the point of the knife, remove and discard the black vein (the intestinal tract) that runs along the back of the prawn.

Mussels

Mussels take moments to cook, but careful preparation is important, so give yourself enough time to get the shellfish ready.

1 Scrape off the fibres attached to the shells (beards). If the mussels are very clean, give them a quick rinse under the cold tap. If they are very sandy, scrub them with a stiff brush.

2 If the shells have sizeable barnacles on them, it's best (though not essential) to remove them. Rap them sharply with a metal spoon or the back of a washing-up brush, then scrape off.

3 Discard any open mussels that don't shut when sharply tapped; this means they are dead and may lead to food poisoning.

Squid

Sliced into rings or cut into squares, squid is a popular fish in Chinese and South-east Asian cooking.

1 Cut off the tentacles just behind the 'beak'.

2 Pull out the beak and discard. Clean the tentacles well, scraping off as many of the small suckers as you can.

3 Reach inside the body and pull out the internal organs, including the plastic-like 'pen'.

4 Scrape and pull off the loose, slippery skin covering the body. Rinse the body thoroughly to remove all internal organs, sand and other debris.

5 Detach the wings and set aside, then cut up the tentacles and body as required. To make squares, slice the body along one side, score diagonally, then cut into squares.

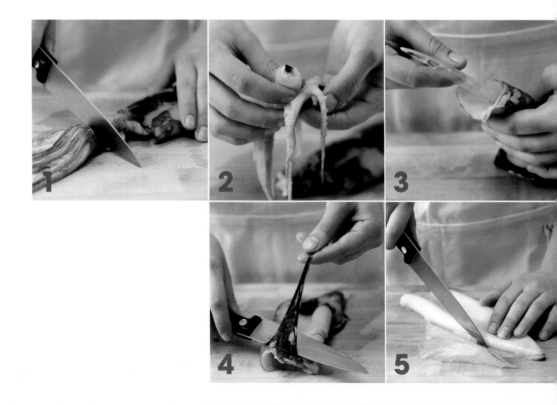

Making stock

Good stock can make the difference between a good dish and a great one. It gives depth of flavour to many dishes. There are four main types of stock: vegetable, meat, chicken and fish.

Cook's Tips

- To get a clearer liquid when making fish, meat or poultry stock, strain the cooked stock through four layers of muslin in a sieve.
- Stock will keep for three days in the refrigerator. If you want to keep it for a further three days, transfer it to a pan and reboil gently for 5 minutes. Cool, put in a clean bowl and chill for a further three days.
- When making meat or chicken stock, make sure there is a good ratio of meat to bones. The more meat you use, the more flavour the stock will have.

Stocks

Vegetable Stock

For 1.2 litres (2 pints), you will need:
225g (8oz) each onions, celery, leeks and carrots, chopped, 2 bay leaves, a few thyme sprigs, 1 small bunch parsley, 10 black peppercorns, ½ tsp salt.

1 Put all the ingredients in a large pan and add 1.7 litres (3 pints) cold water. Bring slowly to the boil and skim the surface.

2 Partially cover the pan and simmer for 30 minutes. Adjust the seasoning if necessary. Strain the stock through a fine sieve into a bowl and leave to cool.

Meat Stock

For 900ml (1½ pints), you will need:
450g (1lb) each meat bones and stewing meat, 1 onion, 2 celery sticks and 1 large carrot, sliced, 1 bouquet garni (2 bay leaves, a few thyme sprigs and a small bunch parsley), 1 tsp black peppercorns, ½ tsp salt.

1 Preheat the oven to 220°C (200°C fan oven) mark 7. Put the meat and bones in a roasting tin and roast for 30–40 minutes, turning now and again, until they are well browned.

2 Put the bones in a large pan with the remaining ingredients and add 2 litres (3½ pints) cold water. Bring slowly to the boil and skim the surface.

3 Partially cover the pan and simmer for 4–5 hours. Adjust the seasoning if necessary. Strain through a muslin-lined sieve into a bowl and cool quickly. Degrease the stock (see opposite) before using.

Chicken Stock

For 1.2 litres (2 pints), you will need:
1.6kg (3½lb) chicken bones, 225g (8oz) each onions and celery, sliced, 150g (5oz) chopped leeks, 1 bouquet garni (2 bay leaves, a few thyme sprigs and a small bunch parsley), 1 tsp black peppercorns, ½ tsp salt.

1 Put all the ingredients in a large pan and add 3 litres (5¼ pints) cold water. Bring slowly to the boil and skim the surface.

2 Partially cover the pan and simmer gently for 2 hours. Adjust the seasoning if necessary.

3 Strain the stock through a muslin-lined sieve into a bowl and cool quickly. Degrease the stock (see right) before using.

Fish Stock

For 900ml (1½ pints), you will need:
900g (2lb) fish bones and trimmings, washed, 2 carrots, 1 onion and 2 celery sticks, sliced, 1 bouquet garni (2 bay leaves, a few thyme sprigs and a small bunch parsley), 6 white peppercorns, ½ tsp salt.

1 Put all the ingredients in a large pan and add 900ml (1½ pints) cold water. Bring slowly to the boil and skim the surface.

2 Partially cover the pan and simmer gently for 30 minutes. Adjust the seasoning if necessary.

3 Strain through a muslin-lined sieve into a bowl and cool quickly. Fish stock tends not to have much fat in it and so does not usually need to be degreased. However, if it does seem to be fatty, you will need to remove this by degreasing it (see right).

Degreasing stock

Meat and poultry stock needs to be degreased. (Vegetable stock does not.) You can mop the fat from the surface using kitchen paper, but the following methods are easier and more effective. There are three main methods that you can use: ladling, pouring and chilling.

1 **Ladling** While the stock is warm, place a ladle on the surface. Press down and allow the fat floating on the surface to trickle over the edge until the ladle is full. Discard the fat, then repeat until all the fat has been removed.

2 **Pouring** For this you need a degreasing jug or a double-pouring gravy boat, which has the spout at the base of the vessel. When you fill the jug or gravy boat with a fatty liquid, the fat rises. When you pour, the stock comes out while the fat stays behind in the jug.

3 **Chilling** This technique works best with stock made from meat, as the fat solidifies when cold. Put the stock in the refrigerator until the fat becomes solid, then remove the pieces of fat using a slotted spoon.

Spices and their uses

Most spices are sold dried, either whole or ground. For optimum flavour, buy whole spices and grind them yourself.

Dry-frying spices

Spices are often toasted in a dry heavy-based frying pan to mellow their flavour and lose any raw taste. Spices can be dry-fried individually or as mixtures. Put the hardest ones, such as fenugreek, into the pan first and add softer ones, like coriander and cumin, after a minute or so. Stir constantly until evenly browned. Cool, then grind, or crush in a mortar and pestle and use the toasted spices as required.

Cardamom, available as small green and large black pods containing seeds, has a strong aromatic quality and should be used sparingly. Add cardamom pods whole and remove before serving, or extract the seeds and use these whole or grind them to a powder just before use. Cardamom is a component of most curry powders.

Cayenne pepper is made from small, hot dried red chillies. It is always sold ground and is sweet, pungent and very hot. Use it sparingly. Unlike paprika, cayenne pepper cannot be used for colouring as its flavour is too pronounced.

Chilli, available as powder or flakes as well as fresh, is a fiery hot spice and should be used cautiously. Some brands, often called mild chilli powder or chilli seasoning, are a mixture of chilli and other flavourings, such as cumin, oregano, salt and garlic; these are therefore considerably less fiery than hot chilli powder. Adjust the quantity you use accordingly.

Cinnamon is the dried, rolled bark of a tropical evergreen tree. Available as sticks and in powdered form, it has a sweet, pungent flavour. Cinnamon sticks have a more pronounced flavour than the powder, but they are difficult to grind at home, so buy ready-ground cinnamon for use in sweet, spicy baking. Use cinnamon sticks to flavour meat casseroles, vegetable dishes, chutneys and pickles.

Cloves are the dried flower buds of an evergreen tree. Strong and pungent, they are one of the ingredients of five-spice powder.

Coriander seeds have a mild, sweet, orangey flavour and taste quite different from the fresh green leaves, which are used as a herb. Sold whole or ground, they are an ingredient of most curry powders.

Cumin has a strong, slightly bitter taste, improved by toasting. Sold whole as seeds, or ground, it is an ingredient of curry powders and some chilli powder mixtures.

Curry leaves These shiny leaves have a fresh-tasting flavour akin to curry powder. They are used as a herb in cooking, most often added whole, but sometimes chopped first. The fresh or dried leaves can be used sparingly to flavour soups and stews. Sold fresh in bunches, curry leaves can be frozen in a plastic bag and added to dishes as required.

Fenugreek seeds are yellow-brown and very hard, with a distinctive aroma and slightly harsh, hot flavour. An ingredient of commercial curry powders, fenugreek is also used in chutneys, pickles and sauces.

Furikake seasoning is a Japanese condiment consisting of sesame seeds and chopped dried seaweed. It can be found in major supermarkets and Asian food shops.

Mustard seeds come from three different mustard plants, which produce black, brown and white (or yellow) seeds. The darker seeds are more pungent than the light ones. Most ready-prepared mustards are a combination of the different seeds in varying proportions. The seeds are either left whole (as in wholegrain mustard) or ground, then mixed with liquid such as wine, vinegar or cider. **English mustard** is sold as a dry yellow powder, or ready-mixed.

Nutmeg, seed of the nutmeg fruit, has a distinctive, nutty flavour. Sold whole or ground, but best bought whole since the flavour of freshly grated nutmeg is far superior.

Paprika is a sweet mild spice made from certain varieties of red pepper; it is always sold ground to a red powder. It is good for adding colour to pale egg and cheese dishes. Some varieties, particularly Hungarian, are hotter than others. Paprika doesn't keep its flavour well, so buy little and often. Produced from oak-smoked red peppers, smoked paprika has an intense flavour and wonderful smoky aroma. Sweet, bittersweet and hot-smoked varieties are available.

Saffron, the most expensive of all spices, is the dried stigma of the saffron crocus flower. It has a wonderful subtle flavour and aroma, and imparts a hint of yellow to foods it is cooked with. Powdered saffron is available, but it is the whole stigmas, called saffron strands or threads, that give the best results. A generous pinch is all that is needed to flavour and colour dishes.

Star anise, the attractive, dried, star-shaped fruit of an evergreen tree native to China, is red-brown in colour with a pungent aniseed flavour. It is strong, so use sparingly, either whole or ground. Ground star anise is used in five-spice powder.

Turmeric is a member of the ginger family, though it is rarely available fresh. The bright orange root is commonly dried, then ground and sold in powdered form. Turmeric powder has an aromatic, slightly bitter flavour and should be used sparingly in curry powder, pickles, relishes and rice dishes. Like saffron, turmeric colours the foods it is cooked with, but it has a much harsher flavour than saffron.

Spice mixes

Curry powder - bought curry powders are readily available, but for optimum flavour make your own.
To make your own curry powder: Put 1 tbsp each cumin and fenugreek seeds, ½ tsp mustard seeds, 1½ tsp each poppy seeds, black peppercorns and ground ginger, 4 tbsp coriander seeds, ½ tsp hot chilli powder and 2 tbsp ground turmeric into an electric blender or grinder. Grind to a fine powder. Store the curry powder in an airtight container and use within one month.

Garam masala – sold ready-prepared, this Indian spice mix is aromatic rather than hot.
To make your own garam masala: Grind together 10 green cardamom pods, 1 tbsp black peppercorns and 2 tsp cumin seeds. Store in an airtight container and use within one month.

Tikka masala – sold ready-prepared as a powder or paste, this spice mix is used with creamed coconut and/or yogurt as the basis of a sauce for chicken, meat or fish.

Food storage and hygiene

Storing food properly and preparing it in a hygienic way is important to ensure that food remains as nutritious and flavourful as possible, and to reduce the risk of food poisoning.

Hygiene

When you are preparing food, always follow these important guidelines:

Wash your hands thoroughly before handling food and again between handling different types of food, such as raw and cooked meat and poultry. If you have any cuts or grazes on your hands, be sure to keep them covered with a waterproof plaster.

Wash down worksurfaces regularly with a mild detergent solution or multi-surface cleaner.

Use a dishwasher if available. Otherwise, wear rubber gloves for washing-up, so that the water temperature can be hotter than unprotected hands can bear. Change drying-up cloths and cleaning cloths regularly. Note that leaving dishes to drain is more hygienic than drying them with a teatowel.

Keep raw and cooked foods separate, especially meat, fish and poultry. Wash kitchen utensils in between preparing raw and cooked foods. Never put cooked or ready-to-eat foods directly on to a surface that has just had raw fish, meat or poultry on it.

Keep pets out of the kitchen if possible; or make sure they stay away from worksurfaces. Never allow animals on to worksurfaces.

Shopping

Always choose fresh ingredients in prime condition from stores and markets that have a regular turnover of stock to ensure you buy the freshest produce possible.

Make sure items are within their 'best before' or 'use by' date. (Foods with a longer shelf life have a 'best before' date; more perishable items have a 'use by' date.)

Pack frozen and chilled items in an insulated cool bag at the check-out and put them into the freezer or refrigerator as soon as you get home.

During warm weather in particular, buy perishable foods just before you return home. When packing items at the check-out, sort them according to where you will store them when you get home – the storecupboard, refrigerator, freezer, vegetable rack, fruit bowl, etc. This will make unpacking easier – and quicker.

The storecupboard

Although storecupboard ingredients will generally last a long time, correct storage is important:

Always check packaging for storage advice – even with familiar foods, because storage requirements may change if additives, sugar or salt have been reduced.

Check storecupboard foods for their 'best before' or 'use by' date and do not use them if the date has passed.

Keep all food cupboards scrupulously clean and make sure food containers and packets are properly sealed.

Once opened, treat canned foods as though fresh. Always transfer the contents to a clean container, cover and keep in the refrigerator. Similarly, jars, sauce bottles and cartons should be kept chilled after opening. (Check the label for safe storage times after opening.)

Transfer dry goods such as sugar, flour, rice and pasta to moisture-proof containers. When supplies are used up, wash the container well and thoroughly dry before refilling with new supplies.

Store oils in a dark cupboard away from any heat source as heat and light can make them turn rancid and affect their colour. For the same reason, buy olive oil in dark green bottles.

Store vinegars in a cool place; they can turn bad in a warm environment.

Store dried herbs, spices and flavourings in a cool, dark cupboard or in dark jars. Buy in small quantities as their flavour will not last indefinitely.

Refrigerator storage

Fresh food needs to be kept in the cool temperature of the refrigerator to keep it in good condition and discourage the growth of harmful bacteria. Store day-to-day perishable items, such as opened jams and jellies, mayonnaise and bottled sauces, in the refrigerator along with eggs and dairy products, fruit juices, bacon, fresh and cooked meat (on separate shelves), and salads and vegetables (except potatoes, which don't suit being stored in the cold). A refrigerator should be kept at an operating temperature of 4–5°C. It is worth investing in a refrigerator thermometer to ensure the correct temperature is maintained.

To ensure your refrigerator is functioning effectively for safe food storage, follow these guidelines:

To avoid bacterial cross-contamination, store cooked and raw foods on separate shelves, putting cooked foods on the top shelf. Ensure that all items are well wrapped.

Never put hot food into the refrigerator, as this will cause the internal temperature of the refrigerator to rise.

Avoid overfilling the refrigerator, as this restricts the circulation of air and prevents the appliance from working properly.

It can take some time for the refrigerator to return to the correct operating temperature once the door has been opened, so don't leave it open any longer than is necessary.

Clean the refrigerator regularly, using a specially formulated germicidal refrigerator cleaner. Alternatively, use a weak solution of bicarbonate of soda: 1 tbsp to 1 litre (1$\frac{3}{4}$ pints) water.

If your refrigerator doesn't have an automatic defrost facility, defrost regularly.

Maximum refrigerator storage times

For pre-packed foods, always adhere to the 'use by' date on the packet. For other foods the following storage times should apply, providing the food is in prime condition when it goes into the refrigerator and that your refrigerator is in good working order:

Vegetables

Green vegetables	3–4 days
Salad leaves	2–3 days

Dairy Food

Eggs	1 week
Milk	4–5 days

Fish

Fish	1 day
Shellfish	1 day

Raw Meat

Bacon	7 days
Game	2 days
Minced meat	1 day
Offal	1 day
Poultry	2 days
Raw sliced meat	2 days

Cooked Meat

Sliced meat	2 days
Ham	2 days
Ham, vacuum-packed (or according to the instructions on the packet)	1–2 weeks

1

Starters and Sides

Basic Pilau Rice

50g (2oz) butter
225g (8oz) long-grain white rice
750ml (1¼ pints) chicken stock
salt and ground black pepper
generous knob of butter to serve

1 Melt the butter in a pan, add the rice and fry gently for 3–4 minutes until translucent.

2 Slowly pour in the stock, season, stir and cover with a tight-fitting lid. Leave, undisturbed, over a very low heat for about 15 minutes or until the water has been absorbed and the rice is just tender.

3 Remove the lid and cover the surface of the rice with a clean cloth. Replace the lid and leave to stand in a warm place for about 15 minutes to dry the rice before serving.

4 Fork through and add a knob of butter to serve.

Serves 4	EASY		NUTRITIONAL INFORMATION	
	Preparation Time 5 minutes	**Cooking Time** 20 minutes, plus standing	**Per Serving** 320 calories, 13g fat (of which 8g saturates), 45g carbohydrate, 0.8g salt	Gluten free

STARTERS AND SIDES **33**

Cook's Tip

- -

Coconut cream is sold in cartons, has a thick creamy texture and can be used in sweet and savoury dishes. Creamed coconut is a solid block of coconut, which can be grated or crumbled into sauces to thicken them. It can also be dissolved in hot water to make coconut cream for this recipe: roughly chop 125g (4oz) coconut cream, add 200ml (7fl oz) hot water, leave for 5 minutes, then beat well until smooth.

Spiced Egg Pilau

200g (7oz) basmati or wild rice

150g (5oz) frozen peas

4 medium eggs

200ml (7fl oz) coconut cream (see Cook's Tip)

1 tsp mild curry paste

1 tbsp sweet chilli sauce

1 tbsp smooth peanut butter

1 large bunch of coriander, roughly chopped

mini poppadoms and mango chutney to serve

1 Put the rice in a pan with 450ml (³/₄ pint) boiling water, set over a low heat and cook for 15 minutes or until just tender. Add the peas for the last 5 minutes of cooking time.

2 Meanwhile, put the eggs into a large pan of boiling water and simmer for 6 minutes, then drain and shell.

3 Put the coconut cream, curry paste, chilli sauce and peanut butter into a small pan and whisk together. Heat the sauce gently, stirring, without allowing it to boil.

4 Drain the rice and stir in the chopped coriander and 2 tbsp of the sauce.

5 Divide the rice among four bowls. Cut the eggs into halves and serve on the rice, spooning the remaining coconut sauce over the top. Serve with poppadums and mango chutney.

EASY		NUTRITIONAL INFORMATION		Serves
Preparation Time 5 minutes	**Cooking Time** 15 minutes	**Per Serving** 331 calories, 9g fat (of which 12g saturates), 50g carbohydrate, 0.6g salt	Vegetarian Gluten free • Dairy free	**4**

Get Ahead

To prepare ahead, fry the aubergine and onion as in step 1. Cover and keep in a cool place for 1½ hours.
To use Complete the recipe.

4–6 tbsp olive oil

275g (10oz) aubergine, roughly chopped

225g (8oz) onions, finely chopped

25g (1oz) butter

½ tsp cumin seeds

175g (6oz) long-grain rice

600ml (1 pint) vegetable or chicken stock

400g can chickpeas, drained and rinsed

225g (8oz) baby spinach leaves

salt and ground black pepper

Aubergine and Chickpea Pilaf

1 Heat half the oil in a large pan or flameproof casserole over a medium heat. Fry the aubergine for 4–5 minutes, in batches, until deep golden brown. Remove from the pan with a slotted spoon and put to one side. Add the remaining oil to the pan, then add the onions and cook for 5 minutes or until golden and soft.

2 Add the butter, then stir in the cumin seeds and rice. Fry for 1–2 minutes. Pour in the stock, season with salt and pepper and bring to the boil. Reduce the heat, then simmer, uncovered, for 10–12 minutes until most of the liquid has evaporated and the rice is tender.

3 Remove the pan from the heat. Stir in the chickpeas, spinach and reserved aubergine. Cover with a tight-fitting lid and leave to stand for 5 minutes until the spinach has wilted and the chickpeas are heated through. Adjust the seasoning to taste. Fork through the rice grains to separate and make the rice fluffy before serving.

Serves 4	EASY		NUTRITIONAL INFORMATION	
	Preparation Time 20 minutes, plus 5 minutes standing	**Cooking Time** 10 minutes	**Per Serving** 462 calories, 20g fat (of which 5g saturates), 58g carbohydrate, 0.9g salt	Vegetarian Gluten free

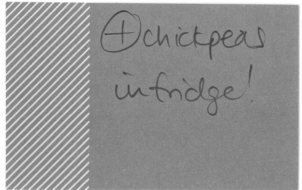

+ chickpeas in fridge!

Curried Coconut and Vegetable Rice

1 large aubergine, about 300g (11oz), trimmed

1 large butternut squash, about 500g (1lb 2oz), peeled and seeded

250g (9oz) dwarf green beans, trimmed

100ml (3½fl oz) vegetable oil

1 large onion, chopped

1 tbsp black mustard seeds

3 tbsp korma paste

350g (12oz) basmati rice

400ml can coconut milk

200g (7oz) baby spinach leaves

salt and ground black pepper

1 Cut the aubergine and butternut squash into 2cm (¾in) cubes. Slice the green beans into 2cm (¾in) pieces.

2 Heat the oil in a large pan. Add the onion and cook for about 5 minutes until a light golden colour. Add the mustard seeds and cook, stirring, until they begin to pop. Stir in the korma paste and cook for 1 minute.

3 Add the aubergine and cook, stirring, for 5 minutes. Add the butternut squash, beans, rice and 2 tsp salt, mixing well. Pour in the coconut milk and add 600ml (1 pint) water. Bring to the boil, cover and simmer for 15–18 minutes.

4 When the rice and vegetables are cooked, remove the lid and put the spinach leaves on top. Cover and leave, off the heat, for 5 minutes. Gently stir the wilted spinach through the rice, check the seasoning and serve immediately.

EASY		NUTRITIONAL INFORMATION		Serves
Preparation Time 15 minutes	**Cooking Time** 30 minutes, plus 5 minutes standing	**Per Serving** 413 calories, 16.8g fat (of which 1.9g saturates), 57.1g carbohydrate, 0.4g salt	Vegetarian Gluten free • Dairy free	**6**

Vegetable Fried Rice

200g (7oz) long-grain rice

3 Chinese dried mushrooms, or 125g (4oz) button mushrooms, sliced

2 tbsp vegetable oil

4 spring onions, sliced diagonally into 2.5cm (1in) lengths

125g (4oz) canned bamboo shoots, drained and cut into 2.5cm (1in) strips

125g (4oz) bean sprouts

125g (4oz) frozen peas

2 tbsp soy sauce

3 medium eggs, beaten

fresh coriander sprigs to garnish

1 Put the rice in a pan, cover with enough cold water to come 2.5cm (1in) above the rice, bring to the boil, cover tightly and simmer very gently for 20 minutes. Do not stir.

2 Remove the pan from the heat, leave to cool for 20 minutes, then cover with clingfilm and chill for 2–3 hours or overnight.

3 When ready to fry the rice, soak the dried mushrooms, if using, in warm water for about 30 minutes.

4 Drain the mushrooms, squeeze out excess moisture, then thinly slice.

5 Heat the oil in a wok or large frying pan over a high heat. Add the mushrooms, spring onions, bamboo shoots, bean sprouts and peas and stir-fry for 2–3 minutes. Add the soy sauce and cook briefly, stirring.

6 Fork up the rice, add it to the pan and stir-fry for 2 minutes. Pour in the eggs and continue to stir-fry for 2–3 minutes until the egg has scrambled and the rice is heated through. Serve immediately, garnished with coriander.

Serves	A LITTLE EFFORT		NUTRITIONAL INFORMATION	
4	**Preparation Time** 10 minutes, plus soaking and chilling	**Cooking Time** about 30 minutes	**Per Serving** 464 calories, 11g fat (of which 2g saturates), 76g carbohydrate, 1.5g salt	Vegetarian Dairy free

Vietnamese Rice Salad

225g (8oz) mixed basmati and wild rice

1 large carrot, coarsely grated

1 large courgette, coarsely grated

1 red onion, finely sliced

4 tbsp roasted salted peanuts, lightly chopped

20g (^{3}/₄oz) each fresh coriander, mint and basil, roughly chopped

100g (3½oz) wild rocket

For the Vietnamese dressing

2 tbsp light muscovado sugar

juice of 2 limes

4 tbsp fish sauce

6 tbsp rice wine vinegar or white wine vinegar

2 tbsp sunflower oil

1 Put the rice in a pan with 500ml (18fl oz) water. Cover, bring to the boil and cook for 20 minutes until the rice is just cooked. Tip on to a plastic tray, spread out and leave to cool.

2 Meanwhile, make the dressing. Put the sugar in a small pan and heat gently until it just begins to dissolve. Add the lime juice, fish sauce and vinegar. Stir over a low heat to dissolve the sugar. Take off the heat and add the oil. Stir into the rice with the carrot, courgette and onion.

3 Spoon the salad into a large bowl and top with peanuts, herbs and rocket. Cover and keep chilled.

Serves	A LITTLE EFFORT		NUTRITIONAL INFORMATION	
6	**Preparation Time** 10 minutes	**Cooking Time** 20 minutes	**Per Serving** 279 calories, 9g fat (of which 1g saturates), 41g carbohydrate, 1g salt	Gluten free Dairy free

Try Something Different

Replace the goat's cheese with two roasted, skinless chicken breasts, which have been shredded.

½ tbsp ground cumin

½ tsp ground cinnamon

2 tbsp sunflower oil

2 large red onions, sliced

250g (9oz) basmati rice

600ml (1 pint) hot vegetable or chicken stock

400g can lentils, drained and rinsed

salt and ground black pepper

For the salad

75g (3oz) watercress

250g (9oz) broccoli, steamed and chopped into 2.5cm (1in) pieces

25g (1oz) sultanas

75g (3oz) dried apricots, chopped

75g (3oz) mixed nuts and seeds

2 tbsp freshly chopped flat-leafed parsley

100g (3½oz) goat's cheese, crumbled

Warm Spiced Rice Salad

1 Put the cumin and cinnamon into a large, deep frying pan and heat gently for 1–2 minutes. Add the oil and onions and fry over a low heat for 8–10 minutes until the onions are soft. Add the rice, toss to coat in the spices and onions, then add the stock. Cover and cook for 12–15 minutes until the stock has been absorbed and the rice is cooked. Season, tip into a serving bowl and add the lentils.

2 To make the salad, add the watercress, broccoli, sultanas, apricots and mixed nuts and seeds to the bowl. Scatter with the parsley, then toss together, top with the cheese and serve immediately.

EASY		NUTRITIONAL INFORMATION		Serves
Preparation Time 10 minutes	**Cooking Time** 20–30 minutes	**Per Serving** 700 calories, 27g fat (of which 6g saturates), 88g carbohydrate, 0.7g salt	Vegetarian Gluten free	**4**

Cook's Tip

Nasi goreng paste can be bought at large supermarkets and Asian food shops.

2 x 250g packs of microwavable rice or 200g (7oz) long-grain rice, cooked, rinsed and drained

1 tbsp sesame oil

6 tbsp nasi goreng paste (see Cook's Tip)

200g (7oz) green cabbage, shredded

250g (9oz) cooked and peeled large prawns

2 tbsp light soy sauce

1 tbsp sunflower oil

2 medium eggs, beaten

2 spring onions, thinly sliced

1 lime, cut into wedges, to serve

Special Fried Rice

1 Cook the rice according to the pack instructions.

2 Heat the sesame oil in a wok or large pan and fry the nasi goreng paste for 1–2 minutes. Add the cabbage and stir-fry for 2–3 minutes. Add the prawns and stir briefly, then add the rice and soy sauce and cook for a further 5 minutes, stirring occasionally.

3 Heat the sunflower oil in a non-stick frying pan, about 25.5cm (10in) in diameter, and add the eggs. Swirl around to cover the base of the pan in a thin layer and cook for 2–3 minutes until set.

4 Roll up the omelette and cut it into strips. Serve the rice scattered with strips of omelette and spring onions, and pass round the lime wedges to squeeze over it.

Serves 4	EASY		NUTRITIONAL INFORMATION	
	Preparation Time 5 minutes	**Cooking Time** 10–15 minutes	**Per Serving** 412 calories, 18g fat (of which 3g saturates), 46g carbohydrate, 1.9g salt	Dairy free Gluten free

Cook's Tip

Thai red curry paste is a hot chilli paste; if you prefer a milder version, use Thai green curry paste.

Hot and Sour Turkey Soup

1 tbsp vegetable oil

300g (11oz) turkey breasts, cut into strips

5cm (2in) piece fresh root ginger, peeled and grated

4 spring onions, finely sliced

1–2 tbsp Thai red curry paste

75g (3oz) basmati rice

1.2 litres (2 pints) weak hot chicken or vegetable stock, or boiling water

200g (7oz) mangetouts, sliced

juice of 1 lime

1 Heat the oil in a deep pan. Add the turkey and cook over a medium heat for 5 minutes until browned.

2 Add the ginger and spring onions. Cook for a further 2–3 minutes. Stir in the curry paste and cook for 1–2 minutes to warm the spices.

3 Add the rice and stir to coat in the curry paste. Pour the hot stock into the pan, stir once and bring to the boil. Turn down the heat and leave to simmer, covered, for 20 minutes.

4 Add the mangetouts and simmer for 1–2 minutes, then stir in the lime juice before serving.

EASY		NUTRITIONAL INFORMATION		Serves
Preparation Time 15 minutes	**Cooking Time** 40 minutes	**Per Serving** 217 calories, 6.5g fat (of which 0.8g saturates), 18.4g carbohydrate, 0.1g salt	Gluten free Dairy free	**4**

Spinach and Rice Soup

4 tbsp extra virgin olive oil, plus extra to serve

1 onion, finely chopped

2 garlic cloves, crushed

2 tsp freshly chopped thyme or a large pinch of dried thyme

2 tsp freshly chopped rosemary or a large pinch of dried rosemary

zest of $\frac{1}{2}$ lemon

2 tsp ground coriander

$\frac{1}{4}$ tsp cayenne pepper

125g (4oz) arborio rice

1.1 litres (2 pints) vegetable stock

225g (8oz) fresh or frozen and thawed spinach, shredded

4 tbsp pesto sauce

salt and ground black pepper

freshly grated Parmesan to serve

1 Heat half the oil in a pan. Add the onion, garlic, herbs, lemon zest and spices, then fry gently for 5 minutes.

2 Add the remaining oil with the rice and cook, stirring, for 1 minute. Add the stock and bring to the boil, then reduce the heat and simmer gently for 20 minutes or until the rice is tender.

3 Stir the spinach into the soup with the pesto. Cook for 2 minutes, then season to taste with salt and pepper.

4 Ladle into warmed bowls and serve drizzled with a little oil and topped with Parmesan.

EASY		NUTRITIONAL INFORMATION		Serves
Preparation Time 10 minutes	**Cooking Time** 25–30 minutes	**Per Serving** 335 calories, 20g fat (of which 4g saturates), 29g carbohydrate, 0.7g salt	Gluten free	4

2

Vegetarian

Curried Tofu Burgers

1 tbsp sunflower oil, plus extra to fry
1 large carrot, finely grated
1 large onion, finely grated
2 tsp coriander seeds, finely crushed (optional)
1 garlic clove, crushed
1 tsp curry paste
1 tsp tomato purée
225g pack firm tofu
25g (1oz) fresh wholemeal breadcrumbs
25g (1oz) mixed nuts, finely chopped
plain flour to dust
salt and ground black pepper
rice and green vegetables to serve

1 Heat the oil in a large frying pan. Add the carrot and onion and fry for 3–4 minutes until the vegetables are softened, stirring all the time. Add the coriander seeds, if using, the garlic, curry paste and tomato purée. Increase the heat and cook for 2 minutes, stirring all the time.

2 Put the tofu into a bowl and mash with a potato masher. Stir in the vegetables, breadcrumbs and nuts and season with salt and pepper. Beat thoroughly until the mixture starts to stick together. With floured hands, shape the mixture into eight burgers.

3 Heat some oil in a frying pan and fry the burgers for 3–4 minutes on each side until golden brown. Alternatively, brush lightly with oil and cook under a hot grill for about 3 minutes on each side or until golden brown. Drain on kitchen paper and serve hot, with rice and green vegetables.

Serves 4	EASY		NUTRITIONAL INFORMATION	
	Preparation Time 20 minutes	**Cooking Time** 6–8 minutes	**Per Serving** 253 calories, 18g fat (of which 3g saturates), 15g carbohydrate, 0.2g salt	Vegetarian Dairy free

Cook's Tips

Chillies vary enormously in strength, from quite mild to blisteringly hot, depending on the type of chilli and its ripeness. Taste a small piece first to check that it's not too hot for you.

When handling chillies, be extremely careful not to touch or rub your eyes with your fingers, as it will make them sting. Wash knives immediately after chopping chillies. As a precaution, use rubber gloves when preparing them if you like.

Bean Sprouts with Peppers and Chillies

3 tbsp vegetable oil

2 garlic cloves, chopped

2.5cm (1in) piece fresh root ginger, peeled and chopped

6 spring onions, cut into 2.5cm (1in) pieces

1 red pepper, seeded and thinly sliced

1 yellow pepper, seeded and thinly sliced

2 green chillies, seeded and finely chopped (see Cook's Tips)

350g (12oz) bean sprouts

1 tbsp dark soy sauce

1 tbsp sugar

1 tbsp malt vinegar

a few drops of sesame oil (optional)

boiled rice with 2 tbsp freshly chopped coriander stirred through to serve

1 Heat the oil in a wok or large frying pan. Add the garlic, ginger, spring onions, peppers, chillies and bean sprouts and stir-fry over a medium heat for 3 minutes.

2 Add the soy sauce, sugar and vinegar and fry, stirring, for a further minute.

3 Sprinkle with a few drops of sesame oil, if you like, then serve immediately with coriander rice.

EASY		NUTRITIONAL INFORMATION		Serves
Preparation Time 10 minutes	**Cooking Time** 4 minutes	**Per Serving** 149 calories, 9g fat (of which 1g saturates), 14g carbohydrate, 0.7g salt	Vegetarian Dairy free	**4**

Asparagus, Pea and Mint Rice Salad

175g (6oz) mixed basmati and wild rice

1 large shallot, finely sliced

grated zest and juice of 1 small lemon

2 tbsp sunflower oil

12 fresh mint leaves, roughly chopped, plus extra sprigs to garnish

150g (5oz) asparagus tips

75g (3oz) fresh or frozen peas

salt and ground black pepper

1 Put the rice in a pan with twice its volume of water and a pinch of salt. Cover and bring to the boil. Reduce the heat to very low and cook according to the packet instructions. Once cooked, tip the rice on to a baking sheet and spread out to cool quickly. When cool, spoon into a large bowl.

2 In a small bowl, mix the shallot with the lemon zest and juice, oil and chopped mint, then stir into the rice.

3 Bring a large pan of lightly salted water to the boil. Add the asparagus and peas and cook for 3–4 minutes until tender. Drain and refresh in a bowl of cold water. Drain well and stir into the rice; season with salt and pepper. Put into a serving dish and garnish with mint sprigs.

Serves 6	EASY		NUTRITIONAL INFORMATION	
	Preparation Time 10 minutes	**Cooking Time** 20 minutes, plus cooling	**Per Serving** 157 calories, 4g fat (of which trace saturates), 26g carbohydrate, trace salt	Vegetarian Gluten free • Dairy free

Get Ahead

Make up to the end of step 2, up to a day ahead. Cover and chill the rice and onions separately.
To serve Complete the recipe.

Oven-baked Chilli Rice

3 tbsp olive oil

1 large red onion, thinly sliced

1 red chilli, seeded and thinly sliced

1 tbsp tamarind paste

1 tbsp light muscovado sugar

350g (12oz) mixed basmati and wild rice

a little oil or butter to grease

20g pack fresh mint, roughly chopped

100g bag baby leaf spinach

50g (2oz) flaked almonds, toasted

salt and ground black pepper

1 Heat the oil in a frying pan and fry the onion for 7–10 minutes over a medium heat until golden and soft. Add the chilli, tamarind paste and sugar. Cool, cover and chill.

2 Meanwhile, put the rice in a large pan. Add 800ml (1 pint 7fl oz) boiling water. Cover and bring to the boil, then turn the heat to its lowest setting and cook according to the packet instructions. Spread on a baking sheet and leave to cool, then chill.

3 When ready to serve, preheat the oven to 200°C (180°C fan oven) mark 6. Tip the rice into a lightly greased, shallow ovenproof dish. Stir in the onion mixture and season with salt and pepper.

4 Reheat the rice in the oven for 20 minutes until piping hot. Stir in the mint, spinach and almonds and serve immediately.

EASY		NUTRITIONAL INFORMATION		Serves
Preparation Time 15 minutes, plus chilling	**Cooking Time** 40 minutes	**Per Serving** 265 calories, 8.1g fat (of which 0.9g saturates), 42.2g carbohydrate, 0.1g salt	Vegetarian Gluten free • Dairy free	**8**

Asparagus Risotto

50g (2oz) butter
2 shallots, diced
2 garlic cloves, crushed
225g (8oz) arborio rice
500ml (18fl oz) hot vegetable or chicken stock
2 tbsp mascarpone cheese
50g (2oz) Parmesan, finely grated,
plus shavings to garnish
2 tbsp freshly chopped parsley
400g (14oz) asparagus spears, blanched and halved
salt and ground black pepper

1 Melt the butter in a heavy-based pan, add the shallots and garlic and cook over a gentle heat until soft.

2 Stir in the rice, cook for 1–2 minutes, then add the stock. Bring to the boil and simmer for 15–20 minutes, stirring occasionally to ensure that the rice isn't sticking, until almost all the stock has been absorbed and the rice is tender.

3 Add the mascarpone, half the grated Parmesan and half the parsley to the pan. Stir in the asparagus and the remaining parsley and Parmesan; season with salt and pepper. Divide the risotto among four plates, garnish with shavings of Parmesan and serve.

Serves 4	EASY		NUTRITIONAL INFORMATION	
	Preparation Time 10 minutes	**Cooking Time** 25 minutes	**Per Serving** 374 calories, 16g fat (of which 10g saturates), 47g carbohydrate, 1.1g salt	Vegetarian Gluten free

1 large rosemary sprig

2 tbsp olive oil

1 small onion, finely chopped

350g (12oz) arborio rice

4 tbsp dry white wine

750ml (1¼ pints) hot vegetable stock

300g (11oz) cherry tomatoes, halved

salt and ground black pepper

shavings of Parmesan and extra virgin olive oil to serve

Tomato Risotto

1 Pull the leaves from the rosemary and chop roughly. Set aside.

2 Heat the oil in a flameproof casserole, add the onion and cook for about 8–10 minutes until beginning to soften. Add the rice and stir to coat in the oil and onion. Pour in the wine, then the hot stock, stirring well to mix.

3 Bring to the boil, stirring, then cover and simmer for 5 minutes. Stir in the tomatoes and chopped rosemary. Simmer, covered, for a further 10–15 minutes until the rice is tender and most of the liquid has been absorbed. Season to taste.

4 Serve immediately with shavings of Parmesan and extra virgin olive oil to drizzle over.

EASY		NUTRITIONAL INFORMATION		Serves
Preparation Time 10 minutes	**Cooking Time** 25–30 minutes	**Per Serving** 264 calories, 4g fat (of which 1g saturates), 49g carbohydrate, 0.5g salt	Vegetarian Gluten free	**6**

Wild Mushroom Risotto

6 tbsp olive oil

2 shallots, finely chopped

2 garlic cloves, finely chopped

2 tsp freshly chopped thyme,
plus sprigs to garnish

1 tsp grated lemon zest

350g (12oz) arborio rice

150ml (¼ pint) dry white wine

900ml (1½ pints) vegetable stock

450g (1lb) mixed fresh mushrooms, such as oyster,
shiitake and cep, sliced if large

1 tbsp freshly chopped flat-leafed parsley

salt and ground black pepper

1 Heat half the oil in a heavy-based pan. Add the finely chopped shallots and garlic, chopped thyme and lemon zest, and fry gently for 5 minutes or until the shallots are softened. Add the rice and stir for 1 minute until the grains are glossy. Add the wine, bring to the boil and let it bubble until almost totally evaporated. Heat the stock in a separate pan to a steady, low simmer.

2 Gradually add the stock to the rice, a ladleful at a time, stirring with each addition and allowing it to be absorbed before adding more. Continue adding the stock slowly until the rice is tender. This should take about 25 minutes.

3 About 5 minutes before the rice is ready, heat the remaining oil in a large frying pan and stir-fry the mushrooms over a high heat for 4–5 minutes. Add to the rice with the parsley. The risotto should still be moist: if necessary add a little more stock. Check the seasoning and serve at once, garnished with thyme.

Serves 6	EASY		NUTRITIONAL INFORMATION	
	Preparation Time 10 minutes	**Cooking Time** 30 minutes	**Per Serving** 340 calories, 12g fat (of which 2g saturates), 51g carbohydrate, 0.9g salt	Vegetarian Gluten free • Dairy free

Baked Stuffed Pumpkin

1 pumpkin, about 1.4–1.8kg (3–4lb)

2 tbsp olive oil

2 leeks, trimmed and chopped

2 garlic cloves, crushed

2 tbsp freshly chopped thyme leaves

2 tsp paprika

1 tsp ground turmeric

125g (4oz) long-grain rice, cooked

2 tomatoes, peeled, seeded and diced

50g (2oz) cashew nuts, toasted and roughly chopped

125g (4oz) vegetarian Cheddar, grated

salt and ground black pepper

1 Cut a 5cm (2in) slice from the top of the pumpkin and put to one side for the lid. Scoop out and discard the seeds. Using a knife and a spoon, cut out most of the pumpkin flesh, leaving a thin shell. Cut the pumpkin flesh into small pieces and put to one side.

2 Heat the oil in a large pan, add the leeks, garlic, thyme, paprika and turmeric and fry for 10 minutes. Add the chopped pumpkin flesh and fry for a further 10 minutes or until golden, stirring frequently to prevent sticking. Transfer the mixture to a bowl. Preheat the oven to 180°C (160°C fan oven) mark 4.

3 Add the pumpkin mixture to the cooked rice along with the tomatoes, cashews and cheese. Fork through to mix and season with salt and pepper.

4 Spoon the stuffing mixture into the pumpkin shell, top with the lid and bake for $1\frac{1}{4}$ –$1\frac{1}{2}$ hours until the pumpkin is softened and the skin is browned. Remove from the oven and leave to stand for 10 minutes. Cut into wedges to serve.

EASY		NUTRITIONAL INFORMATION		Serves
Preparation Time about 40 minutes	**Cooking Time** $1\frac{1}{4}$ hours–1 hour 50 minutes, plus standing	**Per Serving** 438 calories, 24g fat (of which 9g saturates), 38g carbohydrate, 0.7g salt	Vegetarian	**4**

3

Beef, Lamb and Pork

Marinated Pork with Vegetable Rice

1 tsp peeled and grated fresh root ginger

2 tbsp soy sauce

2 tbsp freshly chopped rosemary

4 rindless pork steaks

150g (5oz) brown rice

450ml (3/4 pint) hot vegetable stock

1 tbsp, plus 1 tsp olive oil

1 red onion, chopped

1 red pepper, chopped

a handful of shredded Savoy cabbage

1 Mix the ginger, soy sauce and rosemary in a shallow dish. Add the pork steaks, turn to coat, then set aside.

2 Put the rice in a pan and pour in the stock. Cover and bring to the boil, then simmer over a low heat for 20 minutes or until the rice is tender and the liquid has been absorbed.

3 Meanwhile, heat 1 tbsp oil in a frying pan. Add the onion, red pepper and cabbage and fry for 10 minutes. Heat 1 tsp oil in a separate frying pan and fry the steaks for 4–5 minutes on each side. Stir the vegetables through the rice, then serve with the pork.

Serves 4	EASY		NUTRITIONAL INFORMATION	
	Preparation Time 10 minutes	**Cooking Time** 20–25 minutess	**Per Serving** 462 calories, 11g fat (of which 4g saturates), 41g carbohydrate, 2.2g salt	Gluten free Dairy free

Cook's Tip

- -

To enrich the flavour, add a splash of dry sherry or white wine to the pan when you add the rice.

Mushroom, Bacon and Leek Risotto

25g (1oz) dried mushrooms

250g (9oz) dry-cure smoked bacon, rind removed, chopped

3 leeks, chopped

300g (11oz) arborio rice

20g ($^3/_4$oz) chives, chopped

25g (1oz) freshly grated Parmesan, plus extra to serve

1 Put the mushrooms in a large heatproof bowl and pour in 1.4 litres (2½ pints) boiling water. Leave to soak for 10 minutes.

2 Meanwhile, fry the bacon and leeks in a large pan – no need to add oil – for 7–8 minutes until soft and golden.

3 Stir in the rice, cook for 1–2 minutes, then add the mushrooms and their soaking liquor. Cook at a gentle simmer, stirring occasionally, for 15–20 minutes until the rice is cooked and most of the liquid has been absorbed.

4 Stir in the chives and grated Parmesan, then sprinkle with extra Parmesan to serve.

EASY		NUTRITIONAL INFORMATION		Serves
Preparation Time 10 minutes	**Cooking Time** about 30 minutes	**Per Serving** 452 calories, 13g fat (of which 5g saturates), 62g carbohydrate, 2.6g salt	Gluten free	**4**

Try Something Different

Instead of the squash, use 750g (1lb 11oz) peeled and
seeded pumpkin.
Instead of the onion, use a fennel bulb.

Squash and Pancetta Risotto

125g (4oz) pancetta or smoked bacon, chopped

1 small butternut squash, peeled and
cut into small chunks

1 onion, finely chopped

300g (11oz) arborio rice

1 litre (1¾ pints) hot vegetable stock

1 Put the pancetta or bacon and the butternut squash
into a large deep frying pan and fry over a medium
heat for 8–10 minutes.

2 When the pancetta is golden and the squash has
softened, add the onion to the pan and continue to
fry for 5 minutes until softened.

3 Stir in the rice, cook for 1–2 minutes, then add
the stock. Bring to the boil and simmer for 15–20
minutes, stirring occasionally to ensure that the
rice doesn't stick, until almost all the stock has
been absorbed and the rice and squash are tender.
Serve immediately.

Serves 4	EASY		NUTRITIONAL INFORMATION	
	Preparation Time 10 minutes	**Cooking Time** 40 minutes	**Per Serving** 390 calories, 9g fat (of which 3g saturates), 65g carbohydrate, 2g salt	Gluten free Dairy free

Risotto with Pancetta and Broad Beans

225g (8oz) podded fresh broad beans

50g (2oz) unsalted butter

1 tsp olive oil

125g (4oz) pancetta, chopped

1 onion, very finely chopped

about 1 litre (1³/₄ pints) vegetable stock

225g (8oz) arborio rice or carnaroli rice

150ml (¹/₄ pint) dry white wine

2 tbsp freshly chopped flat-leafed parsley

1 tbsp freshly chopped tarragon

salt and ground black pepper

freshly shaved Parmesan to serve

1 Add the broad beans to a pan of lightly salted boiling water and cook for about 4 minutes until just tender. Drain and refresh under cold running water, then slip the beans out of their skins. Put the beans to one side.

2 Melt half the butter with the oil in a large pan. dd the pancetta and cook until golden, then add the onion and cook gently for 5 minutes or until softened and translucent, stirring from time to time. Meanwhile, bring the stock to a steady, low simmer in another pan.

3 Add the rice to the onion and stir well to ensure that all the grains are coated in butter. Pour in the wine and continue to stir over a low heat as it evaporates.

4 Add the stock a little at a time, allowing the rice to absorb the liquid after each addition. This should take about 25 minutes.

5 Remove from the heat and gently stir in the broad beans and remaining butter. Season with pepper and a little salt if needed, then stir in the parsley and tarragon. Serve immediately, topped with Parmesan.

EASY		NUTRITIONAL INFORMATION		Serves
Preparation Time 15 minutes	**Cooking Time** 35 minutes	**Per Serving** 466 calories, 19g fat (of which 9g saturates), 53g carbohydrate, 1.3g salt	Gluten free	**4**

Lamb and Bamboo Shoot Red Curry

2 tbsp sunflower oil

1 large onion, cut into wedges

2 garlic cloves, finely chopped

450g (1lb) lean boneless lamb, cut into 3cm (1¼in) cubes

2 tbsp Thai red curry paste

150ml (¼ pint) lamb or beef stock

2 tbsp Thai fish sauce

2 tsp soft brown sugar

200g can bamboo shoots, drained and thinly sliced

1 red pepper, seeded and thinly sliced

2 tbsp freshly chopped mint

1 tbsp freshly chopped basil

25g (1oz) unsalted peanuts and toasted

rice to serve

1 Heat the oil in a wok or large frying pan, add the onion and garlic and fry over a medium heat for 5 minutes.

2 Add the lamb and curry paste and stir-fry for 5 minutes. Add the stock, fish sauce and sugar. Bring to the boil, then lower the heat, cover and simmer gently for 20 minutes.

3 Stir the bamboo shoots, red pepper and herbs into the curry and cook, uncovered, for a further 10 minutes. Stir in the peanuts and serve immediately, with rice.

Serves 4	EASY		NUTRITIONAL INFORMATION	
	Preparation Time 10 minutes	**Cooking Time** 45 minutes	**Per Serving** 397 calories, 25g fat (of which 8g saturates), 17g carbohydrate, 0.4g salt	Gluten free Dairy free

2 tbsp light soy sauce

2 tbsp dry sherry

2 garlic cloves, crushed

5cm (2in) piece fresh root ginger, peeled and grated

1 tsp cornflour

450g (1lb) pork tenderloin, cut into thin slices

1 tbsp groundnut oil

1 large carrot, cut into matchsticks

225g (8oz) broccoli, cut into small florets

8 spring onions, shredded

150g (5oz) bean sprouts

salt and ground black pepper

rice to serve

Pork and Vegetable Stir-fry

1 Put 1 tbsp soy sauce, 1 tbsp sherry, the garlic, ginger and cornflour in a large bowl and mix well. Add the pork to the soy sauce mixture and stir thoroughly, then set aside to marinate for 15 minutes.

2 Heat a wok or large non-stick frying pan until very hot and add the groundnut oil. Stir-fry the pork slices in two batches, cooking each batch for 2–3 minutes until the meat is browned. Set aside and keep warm.

3 Reheat the pan, then add the carrot and broccoli and stir-fry for 5 minutes. Add the remaining sherry and soy sauce and 4 tbsp cold water and bring just to the boil. Return the pork to the pan and stir-fry for 2–3 minutes until heated through. Add the spring onions and bean sprouts and stir-fry for 1 minute. Season with salt and pepper, then serve with rice.

EASY		NUTRITIONAL INFORMATION		Serves
Preparation Time 15 minutes, plus 15 minutes marinating	**Cooking Time** about 15 minutes	**Per Serving** 220 calories, 8g fat (of which 2g saturates), 7g carbohydrate, 1.6g salt	Dairy free	**4**

Cook's Tip

Bruise the chillies by pressing them under a heavy, flat-bladed knife.

4 cloves
1 tsp coriander seeds
1 tsp cumin seeds
seeds from 3 cardamom pods
2 garlic cloves, roughly chopped
2.5cm (1in) piece fresh root ginger, peeled and roughly chopped
1 small onion, roughly chopped
2 tbsp sunflower oil
1 tbsp sesame oil
1 tbsp Thai red curry paste
1 tsp ground turmeric
450g (1lb) sirloin steak, cut into 3cm (1¼in) cubes
225g (8oz) potatoes, peeled and quartered
4 tomatoes, quartered
1 tsp sugar
1 tbsp light soy sauce
300ml (½ pint) coconut milk
150ml (¼ pint) beef stock
4 red chillies, bruised (see Cook's Tip)
50g (2oz) cashew nuts
whole chillies to garnish
rice and stir-fried green vegetables to serve

Thai Beef Curry

1 Put the cloves, coriander, cumin and cardamom seeds into a small heavy-based frying pan over a high heat for 1–2 minutes until the spices release their aroma. Leave to cool slightly, then grind to a powder in a spice grinder or blender.

2 Purée the garlic, ginger and onion in a blender or food processor to form a smooth paste. Heat the two oils together in a deep frying pan. Add the onion purée and the curry paste and stir-fry for 5 minutes, then add the roasted ground spices and the turmeric and fry for 5 minutes.

3 Add the beef to the pan and fry for 5 minutes until browned on all sides. Add all the remaining ingredients, except the cashew nuts. Bring to the boil, then reduce the heat, cover the pan and simmer gently for 20–25 minutes until the beef is tender and the potatoes are cooked.

4 Stir in the cashew nuts, garnish with a chilli and serve the curry with plain boiled rice and stir-fried vegetables.

Serves 4	EASY		NUTRITIONAL INFORMATION	
	Preparation Time 30 minutes	**Cooking Time** 40–45 minutes	**Per Serving** 484 calories, 27.3g fat (of which 7g saturates), 29.1g carbohydrate, 1.1g salt	Gluten free Dairy free

Lamb, Potato and Peanut Curry

2 tbsp olive oil
1 medium onion, chopped
1 tbsp peeled and grated fresh root ginger
1.6kg (3½lb) leg of lamb, diced
3–4 tbsp Massaman paste
1 tbsp fish sauce
2 tbsp peanut butter
100g (3½oz) ground almonds
400ml can coconut milk
600ml (1 pint) hot chicken stock
1–2 tbsp dry sherry
500g (1lb 2oz) small potatoes, peeled and quartered
200g (7oz) green beans, trimmed
75g (3oz) toasted peanuts, roughly chopped
20g pack fresh coriander, finely chopped
rice and 2 limes, quartered, to serve

1 Preheat the oven to 170°C (150°C fan oven) mark 3. Heat the oil in a large flameproof casserole. Add the onion and cook over a medium heat for 7–8 minutes until golden. Add the ginger and cook for 1 minute. Spoon the onion mixture out of the pan and set aside. Add the lamb and fry in batches until browned. Set aside.

2 Add the Massaman paste, fish sauce and peanut butter to the casserole dish and fry for 2–3 minutes, then add the reserved onion and ginger mixture, lamb pieces, the ground almonds, coconut milk, stock and sherry.

3 Bring to the boil, then cover with a lid and cook in the oven for 1 hour. Add the potatoes and cook for a further 40 minutes, uncovered, adding the green beans for the last 20 minutes. Garnish the curry with toasted peanuts and coriander. Serve with freshly cooked rice and lime wedges to squeeze over the curry.

EASY		NUTRITIONAL INFORMATION		Serves
Preparation Time 20 minutes	**Cooking Time** about 2 hours	**Per Serving** 664 calories, 47g fat (of which 20.4g saturates), 19g carbohydrate, 0.5g salt	Gluten free Dairy free	**8**

Cook's Tip

Jambalaya is a rice-based dish from Louisiana that traditionally contains spicy sausage, chicken, ham or prawns and lots of chilli pepper.

Beef Jambalaya

275g (10oz) fillet steak, cut into thin strips

4 tsp mild chilli powder

1 tsp ground black pepper

about 5 tbsp oil

150g (5oz) chorizo sausage, sliced and cut into strips, or 125g (4oz) cubed

2 celery sticks, cut into 5cm (2in) strips

2 red peppers, seeded and cut into 5cm (2in) strips

150g (5oz) onions, roughly chopped

2 garlic cloves, crushed

275g (10oz) long-grain white rice

1 tbsp tomato purée

1 tbsp ground ginger

2 tsp Cajun spice mix

900ml (1½ pints) beef stock

8 large cooked prawns, peeled and deveined

salt

mixed salad to serve

1 Put the steak into a plastic bag with 1 tsp chilli powder and the black pepper, seal and shake to mix.

2 Heat 1 tbsp oil in a large heavy-based frying pan and cook the chorizo until golden. Add the celery and red peppers to the pan and cook for 3–4 minutes until just beginning to soften and brown. Remove from the pan and put to one side. Add 2 tbsp oil to the pan and fry the steak in batches; put to one side and keep warm.

3 Add a little more oil to the pan, if needed, and cook the onions until transparent. Add the garlic, rice, tomato purée, remaining chilli powder, ground ginger and Cajun spice mix, then cook for 2 minutes or until the rice turns translucent. Stir in the stock, season with salt and bring to the boil. Reduce the heat, cover the pan and simmer for about 20 minutes, stirring occasionally, or until the rice is tender and most of the liquid has been absorbed (add a little more water during cooking if needed).

4 Add the reserved steak, chorizo, red peppers and celery and the prawns. Heat gently, stirring, until piping hot. Adjust the seasoning and serve with a mixed salad.

Serves 4	EASY		NUTRITIONAL INFORMATION	
	Preparation Time 10 minutes	Cooking Time 40 minutes	Per Serving 554 calories, 30g fat (of which 9g saturates), 40g carbohydrate, 1.8g salt	Gluten free Dairy free

Try Something Different

Use turkey or veal escalopes instead of pork.

Pork, Garlic and Basil Risotto

150g (5oz) Parma ham (6 slices)

6 thin pork escalopes, if necessary pounded with a rolling pin until wafer-thin

6 fresh basil leaves

25g (1oz) plain flour

about 75g (3oz) unsalted butter

175g (6oz) onions, finely chopped

2 garlic cloves, crushed

225g (8oz) arborio rice

450ml (³/₄ pint) dry white wine

450ml (³/₄ pint) hot chicken stock

3 tbsp pesto sauce

50g (2oz) Parmesan, freshly grated

4 tbsp freshly chopped flat-leafed parsley

salt and ground black pepper

1 Preheat the oven to 180°C (160°C fan oven) mark 4. Lay a slice of Parma ham on each escalope and put a basil leaf on top. Fix in place with a wooden cocktail stick. Season and dip in the flour. Dust off any excess.

2 Melt a knob of the butter in a deep ovenproof pan. Fry the escalopes in batches for 2–3 minutes on each side until lightly golden. Melt a little butter for each batch. You will need about half the butter. Remove the escalopes, cover and keep warm in the oven.

3 Melt about another 25g (1oz) of the butter in the pan and fry the onions for about 10 minutes until soft and golden. Add the garlic and rice and stir well. Add the wine and stock. Bring to the boil, then put in the oven and cook, uncovered, for 20 minutes.

4 Stir in the pesto, Parmesan and parsley. Put the browned escalopes on to the rice, cover and put the pan back in the oven for a further 5 minutes or until the rice has completely absorbed the liquid and the escalopes are cooked through and piping hot.

Serves 6	EASY		NUTRITIONAL INFORMATION	
	Preparation Time 15 minutes	**Cooking Time** 50 minutes	**Per Serving** 431 calories, 18g fat (of which 6g saturates), 28g carbohydrate, 0.7g salt	Gluten free

175–225g (6–8oz) rump steak, cut into thin strips

2 tbsp oyster sauce

2 tbsp dry sherry

25g (1oz) dried black or shiitake mushrooms soaked in boiling water for 30 minutes

2 tbsp vegetable oil

1 small onion, thinly sliced

1 garlic clove, crushed

2.5cm (1in) piece fresh root ginger, peeled and cut into thin strips

2 carrots, cut into matchsticks

2 tsp cornflour

salt and ground black pepper

Beef with Mushrooms and Oyster Sauce

1 Put the steak, oyster sauce and sherry in a bowl and add salt and pepper to taste. Stir well to mix, then cover and marinate in the refrigerator for 30 minutes. Drain the mushrooms and reserve the soaking liquid. Squeeze the mushrooms dry; discard any hard stalks.

2 Heat the oil in a wok or large frying pan. Add the onion and garlic and stir-fry gently for about 5 minutes until soft but not coloured.

3 Add the mushrooms, ginger and carrots to the pan and stir-fry over medium heat for about 6 minutes until slightly softened. Remove the vegetables with a slotted spoon and set aside.

4 Add the beef and marinade to the pan and stir-fry for 2–3 minutes, until the beef is tender. Mix the cornflour with 4 tbsp of the soaking water from the mushrooms. Pour the mixture into the pan, put the vegetables back in and stir-fry until the sauce is thickened. Taste and adjust the seasoning with salt and pepper, if necessary. Serve immediately.

EASY		NUTRITIONAL INFORMATION		Serves
Preparation Time 15 minutes, plus soaking and marinating	**Cooking Time** about 15 minutes	**Per Serving** 390 calories, 22g fat (of which 6g saturates), 19g carbohydrate, 0.9g salt	Dairy free	**2**

4

Chicken and Poultry

Spanish Chicken

1 tsp ground turmeric

1.1 litres (2 pints) hot chicken stock

2 tbsp vegetable oil

4 boneless, skinless chicken thighs, roughly diced

1 onion, chopped

1 red pepper, seeded and sliced

50g (2oz) chorizo sausage, diced

2 garlic cloves, crushed

300g (11oz) long-grain rice

125g (4oz) frozen peas

salt and ground black pepper

3 tbsp freshly chopped flat-leafed parsley to garnish

crusty bread to serve

1 Add the turmeric to the hot stock and leave to infuse for at least 5 minutes. Meanwhile, heat the oil in a large frying pan over a medium heat. Add the chicken and fry for 10 minutes or until golden, then transfer to the slow cooker.

2 Add the onion to the pan and cook over a medium heat for 5 minutes or until soft. Add the red pepper and chorizo and cook for a further 5 minutes, then add the garlic and cook for 1 minute.

3 Add the rice and mix well. Pour in the stock and peas and season, then transfer to the slow cooker and stir together. Cover and cook on Low for 1–2 hours until the rice is tender and the chicken is cooked through.

4 Check the seasoning and garnish with the parsley. Serve with some crusty bread.

Without a Slow Cooker

Complete step 1, setting the chicken aside on a plate. At the end of step 2, return the chicken to the pan, add the rice and one-third of the stock, then mix well and simmer until the liquid has been absorbed. Add the rest of the stock, along with the peas, bring to the boil, then reduce the heat to low and cook for 15–20 minutes until no liquid remains. Complete step 4 to finish the recipe.

EASY		NUTRITIONAL INFORMATION		Serves
Preparation Time 25 minutes, plus infusing	**Cooking Time** 20 minutes in pan then 1–2 hours on Low	**Per Serving** 671 calories, 28g fat (of which 5g saturates), 70g carbohydrate, 0.8g salt	Gluten free Dairy free	4

Spiced Chicken Pilau

50g (2oz) pinenuts

2 tbsp olive oil

2 onions, sliced

2 garlic cloves, crushed

2 tbsp medium curry powder

6 boneless, skinless chicken thighs or 450g (1lb) skinless cooked chicken, cut into strips

350g (12oz) American easy-cook rice

2 tsp salt

pinch of saffron threads

50g (2oz) sultanas

225g (8oz) ripe tomatoes, roughly chopped

1 Spread the pinenuts over a baking sheet and toast under a hot grill until golden brown, turning them frequently. Put to one side.

2 Heat the oil in a large heavy-based pan over a medium heat. Add the onions and garlic and cook for 5 minutes until soft. Remove half the onion mixture and put to one side.

3 Add the curry powder and cook for 1 minute, then add the chicken and stir. Cook for 10 minutes if the meat is raw, or for 4 minutes if you're using cooked chicken, stirring from time to time until browned.

4 Add the rice, stir to coat in the oil, then add 900ml (1½ pints) boiling water, the salt and saffron. Cover and bring to the boil. Reduce the heat to low and cook for 20 minutes or until the rice is tender and most of the liquid has been absorbed. Stir in the reserved onion mixture, the sultanas, tomatoes and pinenuts. Cook for 5 minutes to warm through, then serve.

Serves	EASY		NUTRITIONAL INFORMATION	
4	**Preparation Time** 15 minutes	**Cooking Time** 35–40 minutes	**Per Serving** 649 calories, 18g fat (of which 2g saturates), 87g carbohydrate, 2.8g salt	Gluten free Dairy free

Grilled Spicy Chicken

4 boneless, skinless chicken breasts
1 tbsp coriander seeds, crushed
1 tsp ground cumin
2 tsp mild curry paste
1 garlic clove, crushed
450g (1lb) natural yogurt
3 tbsp freshly chopped coriander
salt and ground black pepper
fresh coriander sprigs to garnish
mixed salad and rice to serve

1 Prick the chicken breasts all over with a fork, cover with clingfilm and lightly beat with a rolling pin to flatten them slightly.

2 Mix the coriander seeds with the cumin, curry paste, garlic and yogurt in a large shallow dish. Season with salt and pepper and stir in the chopped coriander.

3 Add the chicken and turn to coat with the spiced yogurt. Cover and leave to marinate in the fridge for at least 30 minutes or overnight.

4 Preheat the barbecue or griddle. Lift the chicken out of the marinade and cook over a medium-high heat, turning occasionally, for about 20 minutes or until cooked through. Serve immediately, with a mixed salad and rice, garnished with coriander sprigs.

Serves	EASY		NUTRITIONAL INFORMATION	
4	**Preparation Time** 10 minutes, plus marinating	**Cooking Time** about 20 minutes	**Per Serving** 157 calories, 2g fat (of which 1g saturates), 3g carbohydrate, 0.2g salt	Gluten free

1 tbsp olive oil

15g (½oz) butter

4 small skinless chicken breasts

lemon wedges to garnish

rice to serve

Chicken with Wine and Capers

For the wine and caper sauce

125ml (4fl oz) white wine

3 tbsp capers, rinsed and drained

juice of 1 lemon

15g (½oz) butter

1 tbsp freshly chopped flat-leafed parsley

1 Heat the oil and butter in a large frying pan over a medium heat. Add the chicken breasts and fry for about 10–12 minutes on each side until cooked through. Transfer to a warmed plate, then cover and keep warm.

2 To make the sauce, add the wine and capers to the same pan. Bring to the boil, then reduce the heat and simmer for 2–3 minutes until the wine is reduced by half. Add the lemon juice and butter and stir in the parsley.

3 Divide the chicken among four warmed plates, pour the sauce over the chicken, garnish each serving with a lemon wedge and serve immediately with boiled rice.

EASY		NUTRITIONAL INFORMATION		Serves
Preparation Time 5 minutes	**Cooking Time** 25 minutes	**Per Serving** 234 calories, 10g fat (of which 5g saturates), trace carbohydrate, 0.3g salt	Gluten free	**4**

125ml (4fl oz) orange juice

grated zest of 1 unwaxed orange

2 tbsp freshly chopped tarragon

2 tbsp freshly chopped flat-leafed parsley

1 tbsp olive oil

1 garlic clove, crushed

4 skinless chicken breasts, about 125g (4oz) each

4 small orange wedges

salt and ground black pepper

brown rice and watercress to serve

Orange and Herb Chicken

1 Preheat the oven to 200°C (180°C fan oven) mark 6. Whisk the orange juice, orange zest, herbs, oil and garlic together in a large bowl. Season with salt and pepper.

2 Slash the chicken breasts several times and put into a large ovenproof dish. Pour the marinade over them and top each chicken breast with an orange wedge.

3 Cook in the oven for 20–30 minutes until cooked through. Serve with brown rice and watercress.

Serves 4	EASY		NUTRITIONAL INFORMATION	
	Preparation Time 10 minutes	**Cooking Time** 20–30 minutes	**Per Serving** 180 calories, 4g fat (of which 1g saturates), 5g carbohydrate, 0.2g salt	Gluten free Dairy free

Try Something Different

- -

Add a drained 225g can of bamboo shoots with the other vegetables in step 2, if you like.

Hot Jungle Curry

1 tbsp vegetable oil

350g (12oz) skinless chicken breasts, cut into 5cm (2in) strips

2 tbsp Thai red curry paste

2.5cm (1in) piece fresh root ginger, peeled and thinly sliced

125g (4oz) aubergine, cut into bite-sized pieces

125g (4oz) baby sweetcorn, halved lengthways

75g (3oz) green beans, trimmed

75g (3oz) button or brown-cap mushrooms, halved if large

2–3 kaffir lime leaves (optional)

450ml (¾ pint) chicken stock

2 tbsp Thai fish sauce

grated zest of ½ lime, plus strips of zest to garnish

1 tsp tomato purée

1 tbsp soft brown sugar

steamed rice to serve

1 Heat the oil in a wok or large frying pan. Add the chicken and cook, stirring, for 5 minutes or until the chicken turns golden brown.

2 Add the curry paste and cook for a further minute. Add the ginger, aubergine, sweetcorn, beans, mushrooms and lime leaves, if using, and stir until coated in the curry paste. Add all the remaining ingredients and bring to the boil. Simmer gently for 10–12 minutes or until the chicken and vegetables are just tender. Sprinkle with strips of lime zest and serve with rice.

EASY		NUTRITIONAL INFORMATION		Serves
Preparation Time 10 minutes	**Cooking Time** 18–20 minutes	**Per Serving** 160 calories, 5g fat (of which 1g saturates), 5g carbohydrate, 1.1g salt	Gluten free Dairy free	**4**

Chicken and Coconut Curry

2 garlic cloves, peeled

1 onion, quartered

1 lemongrass stalk, halved

2.5cm (1in) piece fresh root ginger, peeled and halved

2 small hot chillies

a small handful of fresh coriander

1 tsp ground coriander

grated zest and juice of 1 lime

2 tbsp vegetable oil

6 skinless chicken breast fillets, each cut into three pieces

2 large tomatoes, skinned and chopped

2 tbsp Thai fish sauce

900ml (1½ pints) coconut milk

salt and ground black pepper

finely sliced red chilli to garnish

basmati rice to serve

1 Put the garlic, onion, lemongrass, ginger, chillies, fresh coriander, ground coriander and lime zest and juice in a food processor and whiz to a paste. Add a little water if the mixture gets stuck under the blades.

2 Heat the oil in a wok or large frying pan, add the spice paste and cook over a fairly high heat for 3–4 minutes, stirring constantly. Add the chicken and cook for 5 minutes, stirring to coat in the spice mixture.

3 Add the tomatoes, fish sauce and coconut milk. Simmer, covered, for about 25 minutes or until the chicken is cooked. Season with salt and pepper, garnish with red chilli and serve with basmati rice.

Serves 6	EASY		NUTRITIONAL INFORMATION	
	Preparation Time 15 minutes	**Cooking Time** 35 minutes	**Per Serving** 204 calories, 6g fat (of which 1g saturates), 10g carbohydrate, 1.5g salt	Gluten free Dairy free

Try Something Different

Replace the chicken with pork escalopes or rump steak, cut into thin strips.

4 skinless chicken breasts, cut into strips

1 tbsp ground coriander

2 garlic cloves, finely chopped

4 tbsp vegetable oil

2 tbsp clear honey

fresh coriander sprigs to garnish

Thai fragrant rice to serve

For the peanut sauce

1 tbsp vegetable oil

2 tbsp curry paste

2 tbsp brown sugar

2 tbsp peanut butter

200ml (7fl oz) coconut milk

Chicken with Peanut Sauce

1 Mix the chicken with the ground coriander, garlic, oil and honey. Cover, chill and leave to marinate for 15 minutes.

2 To make the peanut sauce, heat the oil in a pan, add the curry paste, sugar and peanut butter and fry for 1 minute. Add the coconut milk and bring to the boil, stirring all the time, then simmer for 5 minutes.

3 Meanwhile, heat a wok or large frying pan and, when hot, stir-fry the chicken and its marinade in batches for 3–4 minutes or until cooked, adding more oil if needed.

4 Serve the chicken on a bed of Thai fragrant rice, with the peanut sauce poured over it. Garnish with coriander sprigs.

EASY		NUTRITIONAL INFORMATION		Serves
Preparation Time 10 minutes, plus 15 minutes marinating	**Cooking Time** about 10 minutes	**Per Serving** 408 calories, 20g fat (of which 3g saturates), 19g carbohydrate, 0.5g salt	Gluten free Dairy free	**4**

Cook's Tip

Scotch bonnets are small but very hot green, yellow or red chillies frequently used in Caribbean cooking.

Caribbean Chicken

10 chicken pieces, such as thighs, drumsticks, wings or breasts, skinned and pierced with a knife

1 tsp salt

1 tbsp ground coriander

2 tsp ground cumin

1 tbsp paprika

pinch of ground nutmeg

1 fresh Scotch bonnet (see Cook's Tip) or other hot red chilli, seeded and chopped

1 onion, chopped

5 fresh thyme sprigs, plus extra to garnish

4 garlic cloves, crushed

2 tbsp dark soy sauce

juice of 1 lemon

2 tbsp vegetable oil

2 tbsp light muscovado sugar

350g (12oz) American easy-cook rice

3 tbsp dark rum (optional)

25g (1oz) butter

2 x 300g cans black-eyed beans, drained and rinsed

ground black pepper

1 Sprinkle the chicken with ½ tsp salt, some pepper, the coriander, cumin, paprika and nutmeg. Add the chilli, onion, thyme and garlic, then pour the soy sauce and lemon juice over the chicken and stir to combine. Cover and chill for at least 4 hours.

2 Heat a 3.4 litre (6 pint) heavy-based pan over a medium heat for 2 minutes. Add the oil and sugar and cook for 3 minutes or until it turns a rich golden caramel colour. (Be careful not to overcook it as it will blacken and taste burnt – watch it very closely.)

3 Remove the chicken pieces from the marinade and add to the caramel mixture in the hot pan. Cover and cook over a medium heat for 5 minutes, then turn the chicken and cook, covered, for another 5 minutes until evenly browned. Add the reserved marinade. Turn the chicken again, then cover and cook for 10 minutes.

4 Add the rice, stir to combine, then pour in 900ml (1½ pints) cold water. Add the rum, if using, the butter and remaining salt. Cover and simmer, without lifting the lid, for 20 minutes or until the rice is tender and most of the liquid has been absorbed.

5 Add the black-eyed beans and mix well. Cover and cook for 3–5 minutes until the beans are warmed through and all the liquid has been absorbed, taking care that the rice doesn't stick to the bottom of the pan. Garnish with fresh thyme and serve hot.

EASY		NUTRITIONAL INFORMATION		Serves
Preparation Time 40 minutes, plus minimum 4 hours marinating	**Cooking Time** 45–50 minutes	**Per Serving** 764 calories, 25g fat (of which 8g saturates), 85g carbohydrate, 1.8g salt	Gluten free Dairy free	5

Easy Thai Red Chicken Curry

1 tbsp vegetable oil

3 tbsp Thai red curry paste

4 boneless, skinless chicken breasts, about 600g (1lb 5oz), sliced

400ml can coconut milk

300ml (½ pint) hot chicken or vegetable stock

juice of 1 lime

200g pack mixed baby sweetcorn and mangetouts

2 tbsp freshly chopped coriander, plus extra leaves to garnish

rice or rice noodles to serve

1 Heat the oil in a wok or large pan over a low heat. Add the curry paste and cook for 2 minutes or until fragrant.

2 Add the sliced chicken and fry gently for about 10 minutes or until browned.

3 Add the coconut milk, hot stock, lime juice and baby corn to the pan and bring to the boil. Add the mangetouts, reduce the heat and simmer for 4–5 minutes until the chicken is cooked. Add the chopped coriander and serve immediately, garnished with coriander leaves, with rice or noodles.

Serves 4	EASY		NUTRITIONAL INFORMATION	
	Preparation Time 5 minutes	**Cooking Time** 20 minutes	**Per Serving** 248 calories, 8g fat (of which 1g saturates), 16g carbohydrate, 1g salt	Gluten free

Thai Green Curry

2 tsp vegetable oil

1 green chilli, seeded and finely chopped
(see Cook's Tip, page 11)

4cm (1½in) piece fresh root ginger,
peeled and finely grated

1 lemongrass stalk, trimmed and cut into three pieces

225g (8oz) brown-cap or oyster mushrooms

1 tbsp Thai green curry paste

300ml (½ pint) coconut milk

150ml (¼ pint) chicken stock

1 tbsp Thai fish sauce (nam pla)

1 tsp light soy sauce

350g (12oz) boneless, skinless chicken breasts,
cut into bite-size pieces

350g (12oz) cooked peeled large prawns

fresh coriander sprigs to garnish

Thai fragrant rice to serve

1 Heat the oil in a wok or large frying pan, add the chilli, ginger, lemongrass and mushrooms, and stir-fry for about 3 minutes or until the mushrooms begin to turn golden. Add the curry paste and fry for a further 1 minute.

2 Pour in the coconut milk, stock, fish sauce and soy sauce and bring to the boil. Stir in the chicken, then reduce the heat and simmer for about 8 minutes or until the chicken is cooked.

3 Add the prawns and cook for a further 1 minute. Garnish with coriander sprigs and serve immediately, with Thai fragrant rice.

EASY		NUTRITIONAL INFORMATION		Serves
Preparation Time 10 minutes	**Cooking Time** 15 minutes	**Per Serving** 132 calories, 2g fat (of which 0g saturates), 4g carbohydrate, 1.4g salt	Dairy free	**6**

Creamy Curried Chicken

25g (1oz) butter

700g (1½lb) skinless chicken breast fillets, cut into bite-size pieces

1 small onion, chopped

4 celery sticks, chopped

2 tbsp each mild curry paste and mango chutney

2 tbsp lemon juice

2 tbsp each Greek-style natural yogurt and mayonnaise

3 tbsp milk

fresh flat-leafed parsley to garnish

rice to serve

1 Heat the butter in a pan. Add the chicken and fry for 15–20 minutes until cooked, then put to one side. Add the onion and celery to the pan and fry for 5 minutes until soft.

2 Stir in the curry paste, chutney and lemon juice and cook, stirring, for 2 minutes.

3 Take the pan off the heat, add the yogurt, mayonnaise and milk and stir well.

4 Put the chicken back into the pan and bring to simmering point. Cook until piping hot. Divide among four plates, garnish with parsley and serve with rice.

Serves 4	EASY		NUTRITIONAL INFORMATION	
	Preparation Time 15 minutes	**Cooking Time** 30–35 minutes	**Per Serving** 435 calories, 19g fat (of which 7g saturates), 11g carbohydrate, 1.4g salt	Dairy free

Try Something Different

For a more intense flavour, fry 1 tsp black mustard seeds with the spices.
Scatter over 2–3 tbsp chopped coriander to serve.

Cook's Tip

This is an ideal recipe for using up turkey leftover from your Christmas meal.

2 tbsp oil

1 large onion, chopped

2 garlic cloves, finely chopped

1 tsp ground turmeric

½ tsp chilli powder

1½ tsp ground cumin

1½ tsp ground coriander

400g can chopped tomatoes

½ tsp salt

600g (1lb 5oz) cooked turkey

1 tsp garam masala

150ml (¼ pint) thick yogurt

fresh coriander sprigs to garnish

rice to serve

Turkey Curry

1 Heat the oil in a heavy-based pan, add the onion and garlic, and fry gently until softened and golden. Add the turmeric, chilli powder, cumin and coriander, and cook, stirring, for 1 minute.

2 Add the tomatoes and salt. Bring to the boil, cover and simmer for 20 minutes.

3 Remove any skin from the turkey, then cut into chunks. Add to the pan with the garam masala and 4 tbsp yogurt. Cover and cook gently for 10 minutes, then stir in the remaining yogurt. Garnish with coriander and serve with rice.

EASY		NUTRITIONAL INFORMATION		Serves
Preparation Time 15 minutes	**Cooking Time** 35 minutes	**Per Serving** 349 calories, 9g fat (of which 2g saturates), 11g carbohydrate, 1.1g salt	Gluten free Dairy free	4

Thai Red Turkey Curry

3 tbsp vegetable oil

450g (1lb) onions, finely chopped

200g (7oz) green beans, trimmed

125g (4oz) baby sweetcorn, cut on the diagonal

2 red peppers, seeded and cut into thick strips

1 tbsp Thai red curry paste, or to taste

1 red chilli, seeded and finely chopped (see page 38)

1 lemongrass stalk, very finely chopped

4 kaffir lime leaves, bruised

2 tbsp peeled and finely chopped fresh root ginger

1 garlic clove, crushed

400ml can coconut milk

600ml (1 pint) chicken or turkey stock

450g (1lb) cooked turkey, cut into strips

150g (5oz) bean sprouts

fresh basil leaves to garnish

rice to serve

1 Heat the oil in a wok or large frying pan, add the onions and cook for 4–5 minutes or until soft.

2 Add the beans, sweetcorn and peppers to the pan and stir-fry for 3–4 minutes. Add the curry paste, chilli, lemongrass, lime leaves, ginger and garlic and cook for a further 2 minutes, stirring. Remove from the pan and set aside.

3 Add the coconut milk and stock to the pan, bring to the boil and bubble vigorously for 5–10 minutes until reduced by a quarter.

4 Return the vegetables to the pan with the turkey and bean sprouts. Bring to the boil and simmer for 1–2 minutes until heated through. Garnish with basil leaves and serve with rice.

Serves 6	A LITTLE EFFORT		NUTRITIONAL INFORMATION	
	Preparation Time 20 minutes	**Cooking Time** about 20 minutes	**Per Serving** 248 calories, 8g fat (of which 1g saturates), 16g carbohydrate, 1.2g salt	Gluten free Dairy free

5

Fish and Shellfish

Prawn Madras with Coconut Chutney

2 tbsp groundnut oil

1 medium onion, finely sliced

1 green chilli, seeded and finely chopped

600ml (1 pint) vegetable stock

450g (1lb) raw king prawns, peeled and deveined

2 bay leaves

fresh coriander leaves to garnish

basmati rice to serve

For the madras paste

1 small onion, finely chopped

2.5cm (1in) piece fresh root ginger, peeled and finely chopped

2 garlic cloves, crushed

juice of $\frac{1}{2}$ lemon

1 tbsp each cumin seeds and coriander seeds

1 tsp cayenne pepper

2 tsp each ground turmeric and garam masala

1 tsp salt

For the coconut chutney

1 tbsp groundnut oil

1 tbsp black mustard seeds

1 medium onion, grated

125g (4oz) desiccated coconut

1 red chilli, seeded and diced

1 Put all the ingredients for the madras paste into a food processor with 2 tbsp water and blend until smooth. Divide the paste into three equal portions, freeze two (see Freezing Tip) and put the other in a large bowl.

2 To make the coconut chutney, heat the oil in a pan and add the mustard seeds. Cover the pan with a lid and cook over a medium heat until the seeds pop – you'll hear them jumping against the lid. Add the grated onion, coconut and red chilli and cook for 3–4 minutes to toast the coconut. Take off the heat and put to one side.

3 To make the curry, heat the oil in a pan, add the onion and fry for 10 minutes until soft and golden. Add the madras paste and green chilli and cook for 5 minutes. Add the stock and bring to the boil. Reduce to a simmer and add the prawns and bay leaves. Cook for 3–5 minutes or until the prawns turn pink. Garnish with coriander and serve with the coconut chutney and basmati rice.

Freezing Tip

At the end of step 1, put two of the portions of madras paste into separate freezer bags and freeze. They will keep for up to three months.

To use the frozen paste Put the paste in a microwave and cook on Defrost for 1 minute 20 seconds (based on a 900W oven), or thaw at a cool room temperature for 1 hour.

A LITTLE EFFORT		NUTRITIONAL INFORMATION		Serves
Preparation Time 10 minutes	**Cooking Time** 25 minutes	**Per Serving** 415 calories, 29.5g fat (of which 17.8g saturates), 14.5g carbohydrate, 1.8g salt	Gluten free Dairy free	4

Prawn, Courgette and Leek Risotto

1 tbsp olive oil

25g (1oz) butter

1 leek, finely chopped

2 courgettes, thinly sliced

2 garlic cloves, crushed

350g (12oz) arborio rice

100ml (3½fl oz) dry white wine

1.6 litres (2¾ pints) vegetable stock

200g (7oz) cooked and peeled prawns

small bunch parsley or mint, or a mixture of both, chopped

salt and ground black pepper

1 Heat the oil and half the butter in a large shallow pan. Add the leek, courgettes and garlic and soften over a low heat. Add the rice and cook, stirring well, for 1 minute, then pour in the wine. Let bubble until the wine has evaporated.

2 Meanwhile, in another large pan, heat the stock to a steady, low simmer. Add a ladleful of the stock to the rice and simmer, stirring, until absorbed. Continue adding the stock, a ladleful at a time.

3 When nearly all the stock has been added and the rice is al dente (just tender but with a little bite at the centre), add the prawns. Season to taste and stir in the remaining stock and the rest of the butter. Stir through and take off the heat. Cover and leave to stand for a couple of minutes, then stir the chopped herbs through it. Serve immediately.

Serves 6	EASY		NUTRITIONAL INFORMATION	
	Preparation Time 10 minutes	**Cooking Time** 30 minutes	**Per Serving** 320 calories, 7g fat (of which 3g saturates), 49g carbohydrate, 1.3g salt	Gluten free

Cook's Tip

The word 'pilau', or 'pilaf', comes from the Persian 'pilaw'. The dish consists of rice flavoured with spices, to which vegetables, poultry, meat, fish or shellfish are added.

Prawn and Vegetable Pilau

250g (9oz) long-grain rice

1 broccoli head, broken into florets

150g (5oz) baby sweetcorn, halved

200g (7oz) sugarsnap peas

1 red pepper, seeded and sliced into thin strips

400g (14oz) cooked and peeled king prawns

For the dressing

1 tbsp sesame oil

5cm (2in) piece fresh root ginger, peeled and grated

juice of 1 lime

1–2 tbsp light soy sauce

1 Put the rice into a large wide pan – it needs to be really big, as you'll be cooking the rice and steaming the vegetables on top, then tossing it all together. Add 600ml (1 pint) boiling water. Cover and bring to the boil, then reduce the heat to low and cook the rice according to the pack instructions.

2 About 10 minutes before the end of the rice cooking time, add the broccoli, corn, sugarsnaps and red pepper. Stir well, then cover the pan and cook until the vegetables and rice are just tender.

3 Meanwhile, put the prawns into a bowl. Add the sesame oil, ginger, lime and soy sauce. Mix the prawns and dressing into the cooked vegetables and rice and toss well. Serve immediately.

EASY		NUTRITIONAL INFORMATION		Serves
Preparation Time 10 minutes	**Cooking Time** 15–20 minutes	**Per Serving** 360 calories, 5g fat (of which 1g saturates), 61g carbohydrate, 1.8g salt	Dairy free	**4**

Try Something Different

- -

There are plenty of alternatives to cod: try coley (saithe), sea bass or pollack.

2 tsp olive oil

1 shallot, chopped

1 tbsp Thai green curry paste

225g (8oz) brown basmati rice

600ml (1 pint) hot fish or vegetable stock

150ml (¼ pint) half-fat coconut milk

350g (12oz) skinless cod fillet, cut into bite-sized pieces

350g (12oz) sugarsnap peas

125g (4oz) cooked and peeled prawns

25g (1oz) flaked almonds, toasted

squeeze of lemon juice

salt and ground black pepper

2 tbsp freshly chopped coriander to garnish

Coconut Fish Pilau

1 Heat the oil in a frying pan, add the shallot and 1 tbsp water and fry for 4–5 minutes until golden. Stir in the curry paste and cook for 1–2 minutes.

2 Add the rice, stock and coconut milk. Bring to the boil, then cover and simmer for 15–20 minutes until all the liquid has been absorbed.

3 Add the cod and cook for 3–5 minutes. Add the sugarsnap peas, prawns, almonds and lemon juice and stir over the heat for 3–4 minutes until heated through. Check the seasoning and serve immediately, garnished with coriander.

Serves	EASY		NUTRITIONAL INFORMATION	
4	**Preparation Time** 15 minutes	**Cooking Time** 30 minutes	**Per Serving** 398 calories, 7g fat (of which 1g saturates), 53g carbohydrate, 0.4g salt	Gluten free Dairy free

Try Something Different

Use cleaned squid or mussels instead of the scallops and tiger prawns.

Thai Green Shellfish Curry

1 tbsp vegetable oil

1 lemongrass stalk, chopped

2 small red chillies, chopped

a handful of fresh coriander leaves, chopped, plus extra to serve

2 kaffir lime leaves, chopped

1–2 tbsp Thai green curry paste

400ml can coconut milk

450ml (¾ pint) vegetable stock

375g (13oz) queen scallops with corals

250g (9oz) raw tiger prawns, peeled and deveined, with tails intact

salt and ground black pepper

jasmine rice to serve

1 Heat the oil in a wok or large frying pan. Add the lemongrass, chillies, coriander and lime leaves and stir-fry for 30 seconds. Add the curry paste and fry for 1 minute.

2 Add the coconut milk and stock and bring to the boil. Simmer for 5–10 minutes until slightly reduced. Season well with salt and pepper.

3 Add the scallops and tiger prawns, bring to the boil and simmer gently for 2–3 minutes until cooked. Divide the jasmine rice among six serving bowls and spoon the curry over the top. Sprinkle with coriander and serve immediately, with rice.

EASY		NUTRITIONAL INFORMATION		Serves
Preparation Time 10 minutes	**Cooking Time** 10–15 minutes	**Per Serving** 156 calories, 5g fat (of which 1g saturates), 6g carbohydrate, 0.8g salt	Gluten free Dairy free	**6**

Try Something Different

Replace the mussels with 350g (12oz) cooked, peeled prawns.

Garlic Risotto with Fresh Mussels

50g (2oz) butter

175g (6oz) onions, finely chopped

4 garlic cloves, crushed

225g (8oz) arborio rice

450ml ($^3/_4$ pint) dry white wine

450ml ($^3/_4$ pint) hot fish or vegetable stock

3 tbsp pesto sauce

50g (2oz) Parmesan, freshly grated

4 tbsp freshly chopped parsley

1.4kg (3lb) fresh mussels in their shells, cleaned

1 Heat 25g (1oz) butter in a large pan. Add the onions and fry for about 5 minutes or until soft but not coloured. Add half the garlic and the rice and stir well.

2 Increase the heat to medium and add 300ml ($^1/_2$ pint) wine and the hot stock a little at a time, allowing the rice to absorb the liquid after each addition. This should take about 25 minutes.

3 Stir in the pesto, Parmesan and 2 tbsp chopped parsley. Keep the risotto warm.

4 Put the mussels in a large pan with the remaining butter, garlic and wine. Cover with a tight-fitting lid and cook for 3–5 minutes, shaking the pan frequently. Discard any mussels that do not open.

5 Spoon the risotto on to four serving plates. Pile the mussels on top, allowing the cooking juices to seep into the risotto, and scatter with the remaining chopped parsley.

Serves 4	EASY		NUTRITIONAL INFORMATION	
	Preparation Time 10 minutes	**Cooking Time** 35 minutes	**Per Serving** 602 calories, 23g fat (of which 11g saturates), 49g carbohydrate, 1.3g salt	Gluten free

1 tbsp olive oil

1 red onion, sliced

2 tbsp tikka masala curry paste

4 x 100g (3½oz) salmon steaks

400ml can coconut milk

juice of 1 lime

handful of fresh coriander, roughly chopped

lime wedges to garnish and boiled rice to serve

Salmon and Coconut Curry

1 Heat the oil in a pan. Add the onion and cook over a medium heat for 10 minutes until soft.

2 Add the curry paste to the pan and cook for 1 minute to warm the spices. Add the fish and cook for 2 minutes, turning it once to coat it in the spices.

3 Pour in the coconut milk and bring to the boil, then reduce the heat and simmer for 5 minutes or until the fish is cooked through. Squeeze the lime juice over it and sprinkle with coriander. Serve with lime wedges to squeeze over the fish and boiled rice or naan bread to soak up the creamy sauce.

EASY		NUTRITIONAL INFORMATION		Serves
Preparation Time 2 minutes	**Cooking Time** 18 minutes	**Per Serving** 276 calories, 18.6g fat (of which 3.2g saturates), 8.1g carbohydrate, 0.6g salt	Gluten free Dairy free	**4**

Smoked Haddock Kedgeree

175g (6oz) long-grain rice

450g (1lb) smoked haddock fillets

2 medium eggs, hard-boiled and shelled

75g (3oz) butter

salt and cayenne pepper

freshly chopped parsley to garnish

1 Cook the rice in a pan of fast-boiling salted water until tender. Drain well and rinse under cold water.

2 Meanwhile, put the haddock in a large frying pan with just enough water to cover. Bring to simmering point, then simmer for 10–15 minutes until tender. Drain, skin and flake the fish, discarding the bones.

3 Chop one egg and slice the other into rings. Melt the butter in a pan, add the cooked rice, fish, chopped egg, salt and cayenne pepper, and stir over a medium heat for 5 minutes or until hot. Pile on to a warmed serving dish and garnish with parsley and the sliced egg.

Serves 4	EASY		NUTRITIONAL INFORMATION
	Preparation Time 10 minutes	**Cooking Time** 20 minutes	**Per Serving** 452 calories, 20g fat (of which 11g saturates), 38g carbohydrate, 3.6g salt

Smoked Haddock Risotto with Poached Eggs

200g (7oz) smoked haddock

50g (2oz) butter

1 large leek, white part only, trimmed and finely sliced

150ml (¼ pint) dry white wine

300g (11oz) arborio rice

1.1 litres (2 pints) hot chicken stock

4 large eggs

salt and ground black pepper

1 tbsp freshly chopped parsley and black pepper to garnish

1 Put the haddock into a dish, pour boiling water over, cover and leave for 10 minutes. Flake the fish into bite-size pieces, discarding the skin and the bones.

2 Melt half the butter in a heavy-based pan. Add the leek and cook gently, stirring occasionally, for 15 minutes until softened. Add the wine and boil rapidly until it has almost evaporated. Add the rice and cook, for 1 minute, stirring to coat the grains.

3 Put the hot stock into a pan and bring to the boil, then keep at a gentle simmer. Add a ladleful of the hot stock to the rice. Simmer, stirring, until all the liquid has been absorbed. Continue adding the stock, a ladleful at a time, until the rice is al dente (just tender but with a little bite at the centre) – this will take about 25 minutes and you may not need to add all the stock.

4 Meanwhile, bring a wide shallow pan of water to the boil. Crack an egg into a cup, turn off the heat under the pan and slip in the egg close to the water. Repeat with the other eggs and cover the pan. Leave to stand for 3 minutes.

5 Before adding the last ladleful of stock, stir in the pieces of fish and the remaining butter and check the seasoning. Heat the risotto through, adding the remaining stock if necessary. Remove the eggs with a slotted spoon and trim. Top each serving of risotto with a poached egg and a sprinkling of parsley.

EASY		NUTRITIONAL INFORMATION		Serves
Preparation Time 15 minutes	**Cooking Time** 40 minutes	**Per Serving** 536 calories, 19g fat (of which 8g saturates), 66g carbohydrate, 2.9g salt	Dairy free	**4**

Cook's Tip

Buy banana leaves from Asian shops.

Get Ahead

Make the sauce up to 4 hours ahead.
To use Gently reheat to simmering point before you add the fish.

Kerala Fish Curry

4 skinless sole or plaice fillets, about 125g (4oz) each

2 tbsp light olive oil

1 onion, thinly sliced

1 large garlic clove, crushed

1 green chilli, slit lengthways, seeds left in

2.5cm (1in) piece fresh root ginger, peeled and grated

1 tsp ground turmeric

1 tbsp garam masala or 12 curry leaves

200ml (7fl oz) coconut milk

1 tbsp freshly squeezed lime juice, white wine vinegar or tamarind paste

salt and ground black pepper

fresh banana leaves (optional, see Cook's Tip), basmati rice and 1 lime, cut into wedges, to serve

1 Roll up the fish fillets from head to tail, and put to one side.

2 Heat the oil in a deep frying pan over a medium heat and stir in the onion, garlic, chilli and ginger. Stir for 5–7 minutes until the onion is soft. Add the turmeric and garam masala or curry leaves and fry for a further 1–2 minutes until aromatic.

3 Pour the coconut milk into the pan with 200ml (7fl oz) water and bring to the boil. Reduce the heat and simmer very gently, uncovered, for 7–10 minutes until slightly thickened – the consistency of single cream. Stir in the lime juice, vinegar or tamarind. Check the seasoning and adjust if necessary.

4 When ready to serve, carefully lower the fish into the hot sauce and simmer very gently for 1–2 minutes until just cooked. Serve on a bed of basmati rice, in deep bowls lined with strips of banana leaves, if you like, with lime wedges to squeeze over it.

Serves	A LITTLE EFFORT		NUTRITIONAL INFORMATION	
4	**Preparation Time** 10 minutes	**Cooking Time** 20 minutes	**Per Serving** 189 calories, 9g fat (of which 1g saturates), 5g carbohydrate, 0.5g salt	Gluten free Dairy free

Cook's Tip

Basmati rice should be washed before cooking to remove excess starch and to give really light, fluffy results.

250g (9oz) basmati rice

8 x 125g (4oz) tuna steaks

5cm (2in) piece fresh root ginger, peeled and grated

1 tbsp olive oil

100ml (3½fl oz) orange juice

300g (11oz) pak choi, roughly chopped

a small handful of freshly chopped coriander

ground black pepper

lime wedges to garnish

Tuna with Coriander Rice

1 Cook the rice according to the pack instructions.

2 Meanwhile, put the tuna steaks in a shallow dish. Add the ginger, oil and orange juice and season well with pepper. Turn the tuna over to coat.

3 Heat a non-stick frying pan until really hot. Add four tuna steaks and half the marinade and cook for 1–2 minutes on each side until just cooked. Repeat with the remaining tuna and marinade. Remove the fish from the pan and keep warm.

4 Add the pak choi to the frying pan and cook for 1–2 minutes until wilted. When the rice is cooked, drain and stir the coriander through it. Serve the tuna with the pak choi, rice and pan juices and garnish with lime wedges.

EASY		NUTRITIONAL INFORMATION		Serves
Preparation Time 10 minutes	**Cooking Time** about 5 minutes	**Per Serving** 609 calories, 15g fat (of which 4g saturates), 51g carbohydrate, 0.6g salt	Gluten free Dairy free	**4**

6

Classic Meals

Saffron Paella

$\frac{1}{2}$ tsp saffron threads

900ml–1.1 litres (1$\frac{1}{2}$–2 pints) hot chicken stock

5 tbsp olive oil

2 x 70g packs sliced chorizo sausage

6 boneless, skinless chicken thighs, each cut into three pieces

1 large onion, chopped

4 large garlic cloves, crushed

1 tsp paprika

2 red peppers, seeded and sliced

400g can chopped tomatoes in tomato juice

350g (12oz) long-grain rice

200ml (7fl oz) dry sherry

500g pack ready-cooked mussels

200g (7oz) cooked tiger prawns, drained

juice of $\frac{1}{2}$ lemon

salt and ground black pepper

fresh flat-leafed parsley sprigs to garnish (optional)

lemon wedges to serve

1 Add the saffron to the hot stock and leave to infuse for 30 minutes. Meanwhile, heat half the oil in a large heavy-based frying pan. Add half the chorizo and fry for about 3–4 minutes or until crisp. Remove with a slotted spoon and drain on kitchen paper. Repeat with the remaining chorizo, then put the chorizo to one side.

2 Heat 1 tbsp oil in the pan. Add half the chicken and cook for 3–5 minutes until pale golden brown. Remove from the pan and put to one side. Cook the remaining chicken and put to one side.

3 Reduce the heat slightly, heat the remaining oil and add the onion. Cook for 5 minutes or until soft. Add the garlic and paprika and cook for 1 minute. Put the chicken back into the pan, then add the peppers and the tomatoes.

4 Stir the rice into the pan, then add one-third of the stock and bring to the boil. Season with salt and pepper, reduce the heat and simmer, uncovered, stirring continuously until most of the liquid has been absorbed.

5 Add the remaining stock, a little at a time, allowing the liquid to become absorbed after each addition (this should take about 25 minutes). Add the sherry and cook for a further 2 minutes.

6 Add the mussels and their juices to the pan with the prawns, lemon juice and reserved chorizo. Cook for 5 minutes to heat through. Adjust the seasoning and garnish with the parsley, if you like, and serve with lemon wedges.

EASY		NUTRITIONAL INFORMATION		Serves
Preparation Time 35 minutes	**Cooking Time** 50 minutes	**Per Serving** 609 calories, 22g fat (of which 6g saturates), 59g carbohydrate, 1.5g salt	Dairy free	**6**

Cook's Tip

For how to make the perfect risotto, see page 23.

Saffron Risotto with Lemon Chicken

zest and juice of 1 lemon

a small handful of fresh parsley

25g (1oz) blanched almonds

1 tbsp dried thyme

1 garlic clove

75ml (2½fl oz) olive oil

450ml (¾ pint) chicken stock

4 boneless chicken breasts, skin on

50g (2oz) butter

225g (8oz) onions, finely chopped

a small pinch of saffron threads

225g (8oz) arborio rice

125ml (4fl oz) white wine

50g (2oz) freshly grated Parmesan

salt and ground black pepper

fresh thyme sprigs to garnish

1 Preheat the oven to 200°C (180°C fan oven) mark 6. Whiz the lemon zest, parsley, almonds, thyme and garlic in a food processor for a few seconds, then slowly add the oil and whiz until combined. Season with salt and pepper. Heat the stock in a pan to a steady low simmer.

2 Spread the lemon and herb mixture under the skin of the chicken. Put the chicken into a roasting tin, brush with 25g (1oz) melted butter and pour the lemon juice over it. Cook in the oven for 25 minutes, basting occasionally.

3 Heat the remaining butter in a pan. Add the onions and fry until soft. Stir in the saffron and rice. Add the wine to the rice. Gradually add the hot stock, a ladleful at a time, stirring with each addition and allowing it to be absorbed before adding more. This will take about 25 minutes. Take the pan off the heat and stir in the Parmesan. Serve with the chicken, pouring any juices from the roasting tin over it. Garnish with thyme sprigs and lemon wedges.

Serves	EASY		NUTRITIONAL INFORMATION	
4	**Preparation Time** 20 minutes	**Cooking Time** 30 minutes	**Per Serving** 830 calories, 44g fat (of which 15g saturates), 50g carbohydrate, 0.9g salt	Gluten free

50g (2oz) butter

1 onion, finely chopped

150ml ($\frac{1}{4}$ pint) dry white wine

300g (11oz) arborio rice

1 litre (1$\frac{3}{4}$ pints) chicken stock

large pinch of saffron threads

50g (2oz) Parmesan, freshly grated, plus shavings to garnish

salt and ground black pepper

Risotto Milanese

1 Melt half the butter in a heavy-based pan. Add the onion and cook gently for 5 minutes to soften, then add the wine and boil rapidly until almost totally reduced. Add the rice and cook, stirring, for 1 minute until the grains are coated with the butter and glossy.

2 Meanwhile, heat the stock in a separate pan to a steady, low simmer.

3 Add the saffron and a ladleful of the stock to the rice and simmer, stirring, until absorbed. Continue adding the stock, a ladleful at a time, until the rice is tender but still has some bite to it. This will take about 25 minutes and you may not need to add all the stock.

4 Add the remaining butter and the grated Parmesan. Season with salt and pepper to taste, garnish with shavings of Parmesan and serve.

EASY		NUTRITIONAL INFORMATION		Serves
Preparation Time 15 minutes	**Cooking Time** about 30 minutes	**Per Serving** 461 calories, 15g fat (of which 9g saturates), 64g carbohydrate, 0.6g salt	Gluten free	**4**

Cook's Tip

Ready-cooked mussels are available vacuum-packed from supermarkets. Alternatively, to cook from fresh, follow the preparation instructions on page 20, then put them in a large pan and add 50ml (2fl oz) water. Cover with a tight-fitting lid and cook for 3–4 minutes, shaking the pan occasionally, until the mussels open. Transfer to a bowl, discard any unopened mussels, and keep the cooking liquid to one side.

Simple Paella

1 litre (1³/₄ pints) chicken stock

¹/₂ tsp saffro threads

5 tbsp extra virgin olive oil

6 boneless, skinless chicken thighs, each cut into three pieces

1 large onion, chopped

4 large garlic cloves, crushed

1 tsp paprika

2 red peppers, seeded and sliced

400g can chopped tomatoes

350g (12oz) long-grain rice

200ml (7fl oz) dry sherry

500g (1lb 2oz) cooked mussels

200g (7oz) cooked and peeled tiger prawns

juice of ¹/₂ lemon

salt and ground black pepper

lemon wedges and fresh flat-leafed parsley to serve

1 Heat the stock, then add the saffron and leave to infuse for 30 minutes.

2 Heat half the oil in a frying pan and fry the chicken in batches for 3–5 minutes until golden brown. Set the chicken aside. Lower the heat slightly. Add the remaining oil. Fry the onion for 5 minutes or until soft. Add the garlic and paprika, and stir for 1 minute. Add the chicken, red peppers and tomatoes. Stir in the rice. Add one-third of the stock and bring to the boil. Season with salt and pepper. Reduce the heat to a simmer. Cook, uncovered, stirring continuously, until most of the liquid has been absorbed.

3 Add the remaining stock a little at a time, letting the rice absorb it before adding more. (This should take about 25 minutes.) Add the sherry and cook for 2 minutes – the rice should be quite wet, as it will continue to absorb liquid. Add the mussels and prawns, with their juices, and the lemon juice. Stir in and cook for 5 minutes to heat through. Adjust the seasoning and serve with lemon wedges and parsley.

Serves 6	EASY		NUTRITIONAL INFORMATION		
	Preparation Time 15 minutes, plus infusing	**Cooking Time** 50 minutes	**Per Serving** 568 calories, 18g fat (of which 3g saturates), 61g carbohydrate, 2.5g salt		Gluten free Dairy free

Chicken and Mushroom Stroganoff

2 tbsp olive oil

1 onion, roughly chopped

2 garlic cloves, crushed

4 x 125g (4oz) chicken thighs, including skin and bones

250g (9oz) closed-cup mushrooms, roughly chopped

200g (7oz) brown rice, rinsed

175ml (6fl oz) hot chicken stock

150ml (¼ pint) double cream

leaves from 2 fresh thyme sprigs, plus extra to garnish (optional)

50g (2oz) baby leaf spinach

salt and ground black pepper

1 Heat 1 tbsp oil in a pan. Add the onion and garlic, cover and cook gently for 10–15 minutes until soft. Remove from the pan and put to one side. Increase the heat to medium and add the remaining oil. Fry the chicken until golden. Add the mushrooms and cook for 5 minutes or until most of the liquid has evaporated.

2 Put the rice into a separate pan, then pour in 450ml (¾ pint) hot water. Cover and bring to the boil, then reduce the heat and cook according to the pack instructions.

3 Return the onion mixture to the chicken pan and gradually stir in the hot stock. Use a wooden spoon to scrape all the goodness from the base of the pan, then stir in the cream and thyme leaves. Simmer for 5 minutes.

4 Remove the chicken, discard the skin and bones and pull the meat into pieces. Return it to the pan. Add the spinach and stir to wilt. Taste for seasoning.

5 To serve, divide the rice among four warmed plates and ladle the stroganoff over the top. Garnish with thyme leaves, if you like.

EASY		NUTRITIONAL INFORMATION		Serves
Preparation Time 20 minutes	**Cooking Time** 30 minutes	**Per Serving** 494 calories, 43g fat (of which 17g saturates), 4g carbohydrate, 0.3g salt	Gluten free	4

Chicken Tikka Masala

2 tbsp vegetable oil

1 onion, finely sliced

2 garlic cloves, crushed

6 boneless, skinless chicken thighs, cut into strips

2 tbsp tikka masala curry paste

200g can chopped tomatoes

450ml (³/₄ pint) hot vegetable stock

225g (8oz) baby spinach leaves

fresh coriander leaves to garnish

plain boiled rice, mango chutney and poppadoms to serve

1 Heat the oil in a large pan, add the onion and fry over a medium heat for 5–7 minutes until golden. Add the garlic and chicken and stir-fry for about 5 minutes or until golden.

2 Stir in the curry paste, then add the tomatoes and hot stock. Bring to the boil, then reduce the heat, cover the pan and simmer over a low heat for 15 minutes or until the chicken is cooked through.

3 Add the spinach to the curry, stir and cook until the leaves have just wilted. Garnish with coriander and serve with plain boiled rice, mango chutney and poppadoms.

Serves 4	EASY		NUTRITIONAL INFORMATION	
	Preparation Time 15 minutes	**Cooking Time** 30 minutes	**Per Serving** 297 calories, 17g fat (of which 4g saturates), 4g carbohydrate, 0.6g salt	Gluten free Dairy free

Easy Fish Stew

2 tbsp olive oil

1 onion, chopped

1 leek, trimmed and chopped

2 tsp smoked paprika

2 tbsp tomato purée

450g (1lb) haddock or cod, roughly chopped

125g (4oz) basmati rice

175ml (6fl oz) dry white wine

450ml (¾ pint) hot fish stock

200g (7oz) cooked and peeled king prawns

a large handful of baby spinach leaves

crusty bread to serve

1 Heat the oil in a large pan. Add the onion and leek and fry for 8–10 minutes until they start to soften. Add the smoked paprika and tomato purée and cook for 1–2 minutes.

2 Add the fish, rice, wine and hot stock. Bring to the boil, then reduce the heat, cover the pan and simmer for 10 minutes or until the fish is cooked through and the rice is tender.

3 Add the prawns and cook for 1 minute or until heated through. Stir in the spinach until wilted, then serve with chunks of bread.

EASY		NUTRITIONAL INFORMATION		Serves
Preparation Time 15 minutes	**Cooking Time** about 30 minutes	**Per Serving** 347 calories, 7g fat (of which 1g saturates), 30g carbohydrate, 0.5g salt	Gluten free	**4**

Chicken Curry with Rice

2 tbsp vegetable oil

1 onion, finely sliced

2 garlic cloves, crushed

6 boneless, skinless chicken thighs, cut into strips

2 tbsp tikka masala curry paste

200g can chopped tomatoes

450ml (¾ pint) hot vegetable stock

200g (7oz) basmati rice

1 tsp salt

225g (8oz) baby leaf spinach

poppadums and mango chutney to serve

1 Heat the oil in a large pan, add the onion and fry over a medium heat for about 5 minutes or until golden. Add the garlic and chicken and stir-fry for about 5 minutes or until golden.

2 Add the curry paste, tomatoes and hot stock. Stir and bring to the boil, then reduce the heat, cover the pan and simmer on a low heat for 15 minutes or until the chicken is cooked (cut a piece in half to check that it's white all the way through).

3 Meanwhile, cook the rice. Put 600ml (1 pint) water into a medium pan, cover and bring to the boil. Add the rice and salt and stir. Replace the lid and reduce the heat to its lowest setting. Cook for the time stated on the pack. Once cooked, cover with a teatowel and the lid. Leave for 5 minutes to absorb the steam.

4 Add the spinach to the curry and cook until it has just wilted.

5 Spoon the rice into bowls, add the curry and serve with poppadums and mango chutney.

Serves 4	EASY		NUTRITIONAL INFORMATION	
	Preparation Time 20 minutes	**Cooking Time** 25 minutes, plus standing	**Per Serving** 453 calories, 12g fat (of which 2g saturates), 49g carbohydrate, 2.4g salt	Gluten free Dairy free

2 tbsp olive oil

300g (11oz) boneless, skinless chicken thighs, cut into chunks

75g (3oz) French sausage, such as saucisse sèche, chopped

2 celery sticks, chopped

1 large onion, finely chopped

225g (8oz) long-grain rice

1 tbsp tomato purée

2 tsp Cajun spice mix

500ml (18fl oz) hot chicken stock

1 bay leaf

4 large tomatoes, roughly chopped

200g (7oz) raw tiger prawns, deveined

Jambalaya

1 Heat 1 tbsp oil in a large pan and fry the chicken and sausage over a medium heat until browned. Remove with a slotted spoon and set aside.

2 Add the remaining oil to the pan with the celery and onion. Fry gently for 15 minutes or until the vegetables are softened but not coloured. Tip in the rice and stir for 1 minute to coat in the oil. Add the tomato purée and spice mix, and cook for another 2 minutes.

3 Pour in the hot stock and return the browned chicken and sausage to the pan with the bay leaf and tomatoes. Simmer for 20–25 minutes until the stock has been fully absorbed and the rice is cooked.

4 Stir in the prawns and cover the pan. Leave to stand for 10 minutes or until the prawns have turned pink. Serve immediately.

EASY		NUTRITIONAL INFORMATION		Serves
Preparation Time 15 minutes	**Cooking Time** about 50 minutes, plus standing	**Per Serving** 524 calories, 18g fat (of which 4g saturates), 59g carbohydrate, 1.5g salt	Gluten free Dairy free	**4**

Rice and Red Pepper Stir-fry

75g (3oz) long-grain rice
200ml (7fl oz) hot vegetable stock
½ onion, thinly sliced
2 rashers of streaky bacon, chopped
1 small red pepper, seeded and cut into chunks
2 tsp vegetable oil
a handful of frozen peas
a dash of Worcestershire sauce

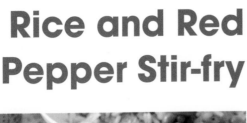
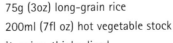

1 Put the rice in a pan and pour over the hot stock. Cover, bring to the boil and simmer for 10 minutes or until the rice is tender and the liquid has been absorbed.

2 Meanwhile, heat the oil in a wok or large frying pan over a medium heat. Add the onion and fry for 5 minutes. Add the bacon and pepper and fry for a further 5 minutes or until the bacon is crisp.

3 Stir the cooked rice and the peas into the onion mixture and cook, stirring occasionally, for 2–3 minutes until the rice and peas are hot. Add a dash of Worcestershire sauce and serve immediately.

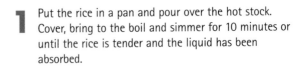

Serves 4	EASY		NUTRITIONAL INFORMATION	
	Preparation Time 5 minutes	**Cooking Time** 15 minutes	**Per Serving** 157 calories, 5g fat (of which 1g saturates), 22g carbohydrate, 0.5g salt	Gluten free Dairy free

Cook's Tip

If you can't find pumpkin, use butternut squash.

Pumpkin Risotto with Hazelnut Butter

50g (2oz) butter

175g (6oz) onion, finely chopped

900g (2lb) pumpkin, halved, peeled, seeded and cut into small cubes (see Cook's Tip)

2 garlic cloves, crushed

225g (8oz) arborio rice

600ml (1 pint) hot chicken stock

grated zest of ½ orange

40g (1½oz) freshly shaved Parmesan

salt and ground black pepper

For the hazelnut butter

50g (2oz) hazelnuts

125g (4oz) butter, softened

2 tbsp freshly chopped flat-leafed parsley

1 To make the hazelnut butter, spread the hazelnuts on a baking sheet and toast under a hot grill until golden brown, turning frequently. Put the nuts in a clean teatowel and rub off the skins, then chop finely. Put the nuts, butter and parsley on a piece of non-stick baking parchment. Season with pepper and mix together. Mould into a sausage shape, twist the baking parchment at both ends and chill.

2 To make the risotto, melt the butter in a large pan and fry the onion until soft but not coloured. Add the pumpkin and sauté over a low heat for 5–8 minutes until just beginning to soften. Add the garlic and rice and stir until well mixed. Increase the heat to medium and add the stock a little at a time, allowing the rice to absorb the liquid after each addition. This should take about 25 minutes.

3 Stir in the orange zest and Parmesan, and season with salt and pepper. Serve the risotto with a slice of the hazelnut butter melting on top.

EASY		NUTRITIONAL INFORMATION		Serves
Preparation Time 15 minutes	**Cooking Time** 40 minutes	**Per Serving** 706 calories, 50g fat (of which 27g saturates), 51g carbohydrate, 1.1g salt	Gluten free	**4**

7

Puddings

Rice Pudding
Fruity Rice Pudding
Vanilla Chilled Risotto

Rice Pudding

butter to grease

125g (4oz) short-grain pudding rice

1.1 litres (2 pints) milk

50g (2oz) golden caster sugar

1 tsp vanilla extract

grated zest of 1 orange (optional)

freshly grated nutmeg to taste

1 Preheat the oven to 170°C (150°C fan oven) mark 3. Lightly butter a 1.7 litre (3 pint) ovenproof dish.

2 Put the rice, milk, sugar, vanilla extract and orange zest, if using, into the dish and stir everything together. Grate the nutmeg over the top of the mixture.

3 Bake the pudding in the middle of the oven for 1½ hours or until the top is golden brown.

EASY		NUTRITIONAL INFORMATION		Serves
Preparation Time 5 minutes	**Cooking Time** 1½ hours	**Per Serving** 239 calories, 8g fat (of which 5g saturates), 34g carbohydrates, 0.2g salt	Vegetarian	**6**

Fruity Rice Pudding

125g (4oz) pudding rice
1.1 litres (2 pints) full-fat milk
1 tsp vanilla extract
3–4 tbsp caster sugar
200ml (7fl oz) whipping cream
6 tbsp wild lingonberry sauce

1 Put the rice into a pan with 600ml (1 pint) cold water and bring to the boil, then reduce the heat and simmer until the liquid has evaporated. Add the milk and bring to the boil, then reduce the heat and simmer for 45 minutes or until the rice is very soft and creamy. Leave to cool.

2 Add the vanilla extract and sugar to the rice. Lightly whip the cream and fold through the pudding. Chill for 1 hour.

3 Divide the rice mixture among six glass dishes and top with 1 tbsp lingonberry sauce.

Try Something Different

Although wild lingonberry sauce is used here, a spoonful of any fruit sauce or compote such as strawberry or blueberry will taste delicious.

For an alternative presentation, serve in tumblers, layering the rice pudding with the fruit sauce; you will need to use double the amount of fruit sauce.

Serves 6	EASY		NUTRITIONAL INFORMATION	
	Preparation Time 10 minutes, plus chilling	**Cooking Time** 1 hour, plus cooling	**Per Serving** 323 calories, 17g fat (of which 10g saturates), 36g carbohydrate, 0.2g salt	Gluten free Vegetarian

Cook's Tip

Orange Poached Peaches Put 100g (3½oz) caster sugar into a pan with 600ml (1 pint) water and the grated zest and juice of 2 oranges. Bring to the boil and bubble for 5 minutes. Add 10 ripe peaches, bring back to the boil, then cover the pan, reduce the heat and simmer for 10–15 minutes until they're almost soft, turning from time to time. Carefully lift out the peaches with a slotted spoon, reserving the liquid. Leave to cool slightly, then remove the skins and put the peaches into a serving dish. Bring the reserved liquid to the boil and bubble for 10 minutes until syrupy. Strain the syrup over the peaches and leave to cool. Cover and chill.

Vanilla Chilled Risotto

900ml (1½ pints) full-fat milk
1 vanilla pod, split lengthways
75g (3oz) risotto rice
40g (1½oz) caster sugar
200ml (7fl oz) double cream
ground cinnamon to sprinkle
Orange Poached Peaches (see Cook's Tip) to serve

1 Put the milk and vanilla pod in a large pan and bring slowly to the boil. Stir in the rice, reduce the heat and simmer gently for 40 minutes, stirring from time to time, until the rice is soft and most of the liquid has been absorbed. You might need to add a little more milk during the cooking time.

2 Stir in the sugar, remove the vanilla pod and leave to cool. Once the mixture has cooled, stir in the cream, pour into a large bowl, cover and chill.

3 Just before serving, sprinkle with a little ground cinnamon. Serve with Orange Poached Peaches.

Serves	EASY		NUTRITIONAL INFORMATION	
10	**Preparation Time** 5 minutes, plus chilling	**Cooking Time** 40 minutes, plus cooling	**Per Serving** 280 calories, 14g fat (of which 9g saturates), 34g carbohydrate, 0.1g salt	Gluten free Vegetarian

Index

Collect the Easy To Makes!...

Good Housekeeping
Slow Cook

easy to make!

Good Housekeeping
Speedy Meals

easy to make!

Good Housekeeping
Chocolate

easy to make!

Good Housekeeping
Chicken

easy to make!

Good Housekeeping
Low GI

easy to make!

Good Housekeeping
Healthy Meals in Minutes

easy to make!

Good Housekeeping
Pies, Pies, Pies

easy to make!

Good Housekeeping
Cakes & Bakes

easy to make!

Good Housekeeping
Soups

easy to make!

Good Housekeeping
Family Meals in Minutes

easy to make!

Good Housekeeping
Wok & Stir-fry

easy to make!

Good Housekeeping
One Pot

easy to make!

Good Housekeeping
Puddings & Desserts

easy to make!

Good Housekeeping
Roasts

easy to make!

Good Housekeeping
Salads & Dressings

easy to make!

Good Housekeeping
Everyday Family Meals

easy to make!

Good Housekeeping
Meat Free

easy to make!

Good Housekeeping
Cupcakes, Muffins and Brownies

easy to make!

Good Housekeeping
BBQ & Grills

easy to make!

Good Housekeeping
Christmas

easy to make!

Good Housekeeping
Pasta & Noodles

easy to make!

Good Housekeeping
Curries & Spicy Meals

easy to make!

Good Housekeeping
Everyday Vegetarian

easy to make!

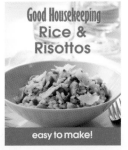

Good Housekeeping
Rice & Risottos

easy to make!

Good Housekeeping
Institute
TRIED ★ TESTED ★ TRUSTED